Tastes of Faith: Jewish Eating in the United States

The Jewish Role in American Life

An Annual Review of the Casden Institute for the Study of the Jewish Role in American Life

Tastes of Faith: Jewish Eating in the United States

The Jewish Role in American Life

An Annual Review of the Casden Institute for the Study of the Jewish Role in American Life

Volume 15

Steven J. Ross, *Editor*
Leah Hochman, *Guest Editor*
Lisa Ansell, *Associate Editor*

Published by the Purdue University Press for the USC Casden Institute for the Study of the Jewish Role in American Life

Production Editor, Marilyn Lundberg

Cover photo supplied by Getty Images, www.gettyimages.com/license/634475051.
Courtesy of Westend61.
Breakfast, bagels, vegetables, salmon and ham.

Cloth ISBN: 978-1-55753-799-7
ePDF ISBN: 978-1-61249-524-8
ePUB ISBN: 978-1-61249-525-5

Published by Purdue University Press
West Lafayette, Indiana
www.thepress.purdue.edu
pupress@purdue.edu

Printed in the United States of America.

For subscription information,
call 1-800-247-6553

Contents

Foreword

Growing up in an Ashkenazi household parented by two Holocaust survivors, our dinners had a rhythm and routine that defined the week. You knew what day it was by what you ate that night: Thursday was dairy night, though much to the delight of my sister and myself, Mrs. Paul's Fishsticks would often substitute for the blander fare of cheese blintzes. Sundays, as was the norm in Jewish households in Queens, New York, we either brought in delicatessen or Chinese food. Every other night was meat—a luxury my parents used to celebrate their more prosperous life in postwar American.

The food Jews eat and the powers of the Jewish palate continue to define the American-Jewish experience, simultaneously serving as points of assimilation and self-preservation. Whereas traditional Jewish food used to represent a resistance to assimilation—a safe haven to preserve a "taste" of the old country in a new world—today it has come to mark a hybrid of identities in the constant fluidity of the American cultural landscape. There is a certain comfort in the familiarity of a *hamishe* matzo ball that the modern assimilated American Jew has come to rely on; or eating in a "kosher-style" deli that represents a safe space in a world that has left traditional Jewish communal existence behind. Even Noah's Bagels, a once kosher establishment, now offers a ham sandwich served on a challah roll. It is as if no matter how far we have deviated from classical Jewish observance, there are still elements of our collective culinary past that we need to survive, if only to remember who we once were before the Holocaust.

This volume explores the role food has played in Jewish life across the centuries: from the humble bagel of the 1500s to the emotionally fraught twenty-first-century meal-time conversations of the fictional Pfefferman family, subjects of the Amazon original series *Transparent*, where serious boundary issues unravel at the family dining room table. Our authors also explore the Jewish origin of the chocolate trade in the Americas; the culinary travails of traveling Jewish peddlers; the rise of Jewish vegetarianism; the meaning of the feast that follows the Yom Kippur fast; and an assessment of how food is interwoven into the very fabric of Jewish identity.

I wish to acknowledge the excellent work of our guest editor Dr. Leah Hochman, Director of the Louchheim School for Judaic Studies and Associate Professor of Jewish Thought at the Los Angeles campus of Hebrew Union College-Jewish Institute of Religion. Dr. Hochman's compilation of articles offers a broad and rich examination of the impact of food has had on the creation and constant redefinition of Jewish identity in America.

The Casden Institute dedicates this volume to Rob Eshman, author of the "Foodaism" Blog, who is leaving the *Jewish Journal* after twenty-three years of service, many of them as publisher and editor-in-chief.

Steven J. Ross
Myron and Marian Casden Director
Professor of History

Editorial Introduction
On Eating and Being Jewish: How Taste Has Shaped Identity

by Leah Hochman, Guest Editor

So goes an old joke about Jews in history: "They tried to kill us. We survived. Let's eat." As stoic as it is pithy, the sentiment reveals a long-standing self-understanding of Jewish longevity, persecution and irony. Chief among its truisms is the centrality of food in Jewish life, culture, and religious experience. Every holiday, every life cycle event, virtually every Jewish gathering employs food as a means of marking connections to seasonal bounty, cultural heritage and religious commitment. Apples and honey (or dates and pomegranate) on Rosh Hashanah, *matzah* on Passover, bagels after the ceremony that welcomes infants into the community, Chinese food on Christmas Eve—name the occasion and someone can name a specific dish that accompanies it. From the food brought by friends to feed mourners in the days following a family member's funeral to the weekly communion with bread at the Sabbath table, Jews and their food are indelibly linked.

The cultural value of Jewish food in American society has a wide range and a long history. As Jews emigrated from Spanish and Portuguese holdings in the colonial period, from central Europe in the eighteenth and nineteenth centuries, and from eastern Europe, the Middle East and the Mediterranean in the twentieth century, they brought with them flavors and ingredients, techniques and textures, trade routes and suppliers. Equally as important, every Jewish immigrant group brought with them an enthusiasm to adapt to their new homeland and incorporate their native food traditions with those of their fellow immigrants and citizens. Over the course of the 363 years of Jewish life in America, Jews have cooked and baked, curated and created, eaten and enjoyed a unique and exceptional American Jewish cuisine.

That cuisine is a startling treasure trove of cultural, social, and historical information. As the French lawyer and gastronome Jean Brillat-Savarin noted in the nineteenth century, "Tell me what you eat and I shall tell you who you are" (21). (In the case of Jews who observe the dietary guidelines of *kashrut*, he might have added what one does not eat as well.) Food, along with all the ways people procure, prepare, secure and serve it, exposes the values and desires of those who eat it. Foodways—the social, religious, political, cultural and economic habits, means and reasons related to eating and producing food—reveal curious and interesting details about cultural and societal tastes (Anderson 156). And those tastes include both flavor profiles (vastly different across Jewish ethnicities and communities) and various senses of refinement and judgment. In much the same way as clothes, hairstyles, and accessories project interconnected signals about a person's priorities and commitments, what one chooses to eat and drink—and how one chooses to drink or eat it—unveils information about identity, self-perception and mores. And while the significance of food in Jewish experience seems self-evident, the role it plays in the construction of cultural boundaries often goes unremarked. The essays in the current volume seek to redress that silence. Stretching from pre-Colonial America chocolate traders and immigrant peddlers to a twenty-first-century Web-based television family, the investigations that follow provide their own rich contribution to understanding and articulating the foodways of American Jews.

It is not just a quirk of American culture that Jewish foods foster a sense of Jewishness even when they do not adhere to the dietary guidelines laid out in biblical text and interpreted, refined, expanded over the centuries by rabbinic thought and innovation. One need not look farther than the Reuben sandwich to prove the point; as a classic American creation it layers corned beef on rye bread with Swiss cheese, sauerkraut and Russian dressing and thus violates the religious injunction to separate meat from dairy. Yet as a staple on Jewish delicatessen menus nationwide, the Reuben gestures toward a set of foodways that are intimately connected to Jewish immigration in the twentieth century, to the American penchant for meat at every meal, to the prevalence of dairy products (Swiss cheese is, ironically, primarily an American invention), and to the ways in which food takes on the flavors and fads of its producers and consumers (Weil). As American Jews assimilated and changed the norms of their religious behaviors, food styles became as important—in some cases more important—than adherence to religious principles.

Indeed, much of what one may consider "Jewish" food has surprisingly little origin in anything specifically Jewish. Many foods recognized or projected as particular to Jewish foodways are regional foods that were brought over from different places around the world. Some of those foods came with the waves of Jewish immigrants in the mid-nineteenth century—foods like gefilte fish, which originates in German speaking countries; poppyseed, which Americans have come to use as a type of garnish or decoration but which remains an integral part of German, Austrian and Hungarian baking; and herring (indeed, all kinds of smoked and pickled fish), which is found throughout Europe and Scandinavia in particular—and became associated with Jews only after they came to the United States. Other Jewish foods immigrated with the over two million Jews who came to the United States between 1880 and 1925 (the majority from Eastern Europe). And still others of those foods considered "Jewish"—by which most people actually mean Ashkenazi—came not from Europe at all but are American innovations.[1]

In contrast to the metaphor of the great melting pot, immigrants brought with them their particular spices and tastes—Galician Jews prefer food sweet, Latvians prefer more savory—their specific products and dishes—paprika and cholent and apple tarts and the myriad of different kinds of dumplings—and their regional preferences—smoked or boiled or fried or baked. And as with other immigrant groups whose signature foodways developed after their arrival in the United States, the style of Jewish food became encoded through repetition in newspapers, journals, radio advertisements, films, cookbooks and corporate sponsored publications.[2] Still today, television, movies, literature, even Instagram project a whole array of unspoken ideas and assumptions about Jewish foods and those who enjoy—and those who reject—them.

Such food coding is not specific to immigrant food; fantastically interesting research has exposed the unconscious assumptions triggered by Starbucks coffee and those who choose to drink it (Kuehn et al.; see also Simon). Similar studies have shown how those assumptions change when that cuppa comes from Dunkin' Donuts (Contois; see also Leist). One need only ask oneself about how one's own judgments and preconceptions change depending on the kind of food served at a gathering or the type of drink a speaker displays (diet soda? tap water? Which brand of bottled water?). The casual exposure of self in the nonverbal expression of food choice allows observers to make suppositions about ethnicity, class, disposable income, and a sense of worldliness based on a product, where that product was purchased and how that choice is displayed. All food choices operate the same way; they offer a fantastic resource for mining all kinds of data about cultural predilections, ethnic mores, and those ideas and symbols that a group of individuals holds dear. Food—what we eat, how we eat it, when we eat it—forms a deep, lasting, often unconscious but also revealing aspect of identity.

For American Jews, and those who enjoy American Jewish foods, foodways are one of the many ways to investigate what Americans think it means to *be* Jewish and what "Jewish" means. Lenny Bruce's classic routine from 1964 makes clear that what is and what is not "Jewish" relies not on theological or religious commitment but rather on a constructed set of norms and food fads. The bit is dated now—and the distinctions he makes still border on (if not also crossover to) offensive—but Bruce's keen eye showcases the foods that distinguished middle American Jews as a separate cultural group. "Kool-Aid," he revealed, "not so Jewish. Pumpernickel, very Jewish. White bread. Not Jewish."[3] That many of the foods he named explicitly no longer carry the connotations on which his routine relied indicates that those boundaries have shifted over time; generations of Jewish eaters have different referents and different flavors by which they shape their identities. Lime Jello is no longer stylish. Even Milton Berle's joke about pastrami on white bread with mayo is dated.[4] But the knowledge that Jewish foodways are completely beholden to the contexts in which they arise and operate contributes to the ways in which they code not just cultural connection but nostalgia, memory and desire. Food has meaning and that meaning is constantly shifting to reflect the values and significance of the society at large. The deep dive into understanding food and the role it plays in the boundaries ethnic groups erect (or dismantle) for themselves reveal how a culture functions in a particular time and place.

The theory of the "culinary triangle" developed by French anthropologist Claude Lévi-Strauss describes a framework by which to identify the foods cultures revere, accept and reject. The three distinct poles of his triangle—raw (wild), cooked (made edible through human intervention and production), rotted (rejected)—expose the foods (and, by extension, cooking processes) that define cultural values and worldviews. Of course, one culture's rotted is another group's cooked. Lévi-Strauss' idea relies on the observation that our assumptions are informed by sensory perceptions and further cultivated by cultural contexts. And those same cultural contexts make it clear that some rotting (or controlled rotting) is acceptable. One knows whether milk has soured because it smells bad or tastes off or curdles when poured; it may seem self-evident to reject it. A culinary triangle allows one to ask about the terms of such a rejection—perhaps economic (for those for whom buying new milk is not a burden) or constructed (for those for whom an expiration date supersedes sensory input)—or its use as the basis of other foods (moldy milk can make a lovely blue cheese). The sliding scale of acceptability and palatability determines and exposes the far corners of cultural boundaries of taste. More importantly, clashes and connections among food triangles reveals ways different cultures combine or rebuff each other's tastes. The sheer elation of Muslim and Jewish children throughout the United States when, in 1997, the Nabisco Corporation finally dropped lard out of its Oreo cookie production process might be proof enough of the power of a single ingredient to include or exclude whole populations of eaters.[5]

Lévi-Strauss offers the valuable insight that the three poles of his triangle are not universals. Judgements about taste, edibility, and disgust change as the values and priorities of a culture mature, widen or narrow. Forty years ago organic food was the domain of do-it-yourselfers and environmentalists; today the market share for organic products and processes has exploded (and been exploited). As globalism has made its mark in everything from condiments to convenience, foods have moved from one category to another with increasing frequency. (When I was growing up in suburban Seattle, for example, sushi was still an expensive, exotic, intriguing but intimidating rarity. Now one can buy it prepacked with packets of soy sauce and a dollop of wasabi in containers anywhere from the gas station to Safeco Field.) Indeed, the idea of "culture" itself is a fluid term. As the dynamic between what members of a group consider edible and inedible changes, different groups and their foodways construct very different triangles. While the cooked represents culture and the raw nature, the ongoing relationship between acceptable and unacceptable shifts as well. Charting that changeability is one of the goals of the current volume.

Food has long been a fascination to me. My maternal family has been on the West Coast for three generations; our gefilte fish was pink (my grandmother used salmon). My closest friends came from Sephardic families whose complicated kinship connections gave rise to fantastic, competing recipes for *biscochos*, *bourekas*, and *boyos* ("b's in the freezer" we called them). As a latchkey kid, I would come home from elementary school and bake elaborate cakes for my family in the time (I think) I was meant to do homework. Though my Pacific Northwest framework included a deep appreciation for the flavors of Japan, I had little experience with the flavors of the Americas; I had no idea of what I had no idea existed. One particularly stark memory comes from ordering my first quesadilla in Los Angeles and being schooled in pronunciation by a classmate. On a trip with my father to his native Brooklyn I encountered other new culinary artefacts—the knish, the pickle barrel, a hot dog cart. By the time I was on my own, eating in the Middle East and then New England, Central Europe and then the Southeast, my gastronomic worldview had exploded and reformed hundreds of times. In graduate school I poured over recipes with ingredients I could never afford; in my first permanent academic appointment, I subscribed to *Gourmet* and cooked my way through every single issue.

All the while I had discovered and deepened an abiding passion for the study of religions. As a high school sophomore I pleaded my way into an upperclass religion and philosophy class; it sparked a burrowing interest that has never gone away. During college I encountered Jewish history for the first time; I can describe the day, the hour, the minute inspiration hit (my beloved professor Allen Greenberg [*z"l*] was unpacking Michael Meyer's 1972 text *The Origin of the Modern Jew*). In all its quirks, innovations and deeply personal rejection of centuries old traditions and knowledge modern identity continues to fascinate and thrill me. It seemed inevitable that I would find the framework that best fit my penchant for interdisciplinary study in a department of religious studies.

Why it took so long to find my way to the academic field that marries food studies with the study of religion remains a mystery. Yet I have been teaching the unmistakable connection between food and religion for over a decade, first at the University of Florida and now at the University of Southern California and the Hebrew Union College-Jewish Institute of Religion in Los Angeles. And when the opportunity came to propose a volume for the USC Casden Institute for the Study of the Jewish Role in American Life Annual Series I jumped at the chance. I offer my deep and heartfelt thanks to Dr. Steve Ross, the Myron and Marion Casden Director, and Lisa Ansell, the Associate Director of the Casden Institute, for allowing me to guest edit this volume. It has been a real pleasure to work with them both and I have been deeply grateful for their continued enthusiasm, close reading, support, interest and patience.

And what a delight to bring together the six essays that follow! Together they bring a very rich and full picture of Jewish foodways from virtually the first landing of Jews on American soil in the middle of the seventeenth century to the third season of Amazon's Web series *Transparent* last year. They are grouped together as complementary pairs detailing important foodways in American trade, immigrant tastes and commitments, and twenty-first-century American habits and nostalgia. Deborah Prinz's clever and enlightening essay on the pioneering role of Sephardi and Ashkenazi Jews in the chocolate trade during the Colonial and Revolutionary War periods is a fascinating exploration of pan-Atlantic kinship and economic ties. Before coffee's dominance and while tea supplies were restricted, drinking chocolate provided nutrition, comfort and much desired prestige that Jewish chocolatiers could amply provide. Hasia R. Diner has explored the many ways in Jewish peddlers navigated and negotiated adherence to the laws and customs of *kashrut* and holiday observances even as they moved across vast territory and often remained the only Jew for hundreds of miles.[6] Her insight into what she calls "situational kashrut" reveals the possibilities and complications of interfaith interactions and the ways in which American opened other boundaries beyond the geographical.

The meticulously researched essay by Jeffrey Marx is a must read for anyone who has pondered the nearly holy Jewish trinity of bagels, lox and cream cheese. In illuminating detail, he has provided a narrative of the happy coincidences and astute innovations that gave rise to the sustained popularity of a *shmear* on a bagel. His insight into the salmon trade alone is enough to warrant a trip to one's local appetizing shop. That care and attention to detail is evident as well in Eve Jochnowitz's study of Jewish vegetarianism in the first part of the twentieth century and the variety of ideological commitments with which primarily Yiddish speaking vegetarians came to their rejection of eating animals. Her use of the artefacts of material culture—cookbooks, gravestones, and comic strips—shows both the dedication of Jewish vegetarians to rejecting meat and the deep threat such a rejection seemed to represent to members of the mainstream Yiddish cultural presses.

Nora L. Rubel's careful and revealing article on the development and rise in importance of the all-American non-liturgical holiday of Break Fast—the meal that ends the twenty-five hour fast on Yom Kippur—showcases the deep and lasting ties between community building and eating even when (perhaps especially when) participants do not observe the fast themselves.[7] She shows the manner in which the richly meaningful relationships between food and religion express themselves for those for whom theology holds less sway than identity and interconnection. And, finally, the essay by Rebecca T. Alpert on the use, function, symbolism and avid love of food by and among the Pfefferman family in the groundbreaking Web series *Transparent* provides a close reading of the culmination of American Jewish eating. She weaves together the nostalgia the Pfefferman parents have with the food of their youth with the deeply conflicted feelings those same parents have about the use of food in manipulating, developing, and fostering familial ties and communal commitments. Detailing how each of the show's characters uses food to express both positive and negative emotions, Alpert offers a close read on contemporary American

Jewish assumptions about their food inheritance, their cosmopolitanism and their ethical conundrums.

In 1966, cultural critic Roland Barthes mused about the role food plays in society. "For what is food?" he asked rhetorically. "It is not only a collection of products that can be used for statistical or nutritional studies. It is also, and at the same time, a system of communication, a body of images, a protocol of usages, situations and behavior" (24). His insight into the way food (and foodways) talks, shares stories and ideas, and provides details about who eats what and when has long informed my own exploration of Jewish foodways. It is my hope that together the essays in this volume will spark in its readers a similar desire to know how food communicates, for and to whom, when, and in what ways. Happily, the foodways discussed in this collection did not come down with Moses from the mountain top; instead they demonstrate the ways in which American Jews have communicated American Jewish commitments, concerns and innovations for over three centuries.

I would be remiss if I did not thank at least some of the people who helped foster my interest in food and Jewish identity. My father Stanley Hochman (*z"l*) was an early experimenter in the kitchen (his creations might not have been met with the grace they deserved) and had a late yet very successful bloom as a third-career baker and cake decorator. My mother Linda Potter Hochman, whose green thumb and deep commitment to horticulture kept us in organic produce well before it was cool to do so, has taken on the role of family food historian and preserved many of the oral recipes my grandparents had perfected. My grandfather, Edward Potter (*z"l*) made the family jam, fashioned the family *hamentaschen* recipe, always made his own lemonade at the table in every restaurant, and repeatedly took great pleasure in relating to me the story of his father tricking his kosher observant mother into eating pork chops (I can still hear him, narrating with glee her exclamation that "these are the most delicious lamb chops I've ever eaten!"). And my grandmother Alice Potter bequeathed to me her mother's Yiddish recipe books, an electric knife with which to cut brisket, loaf pans to make proper *kamish broit*, and a deep love of and appreciation for the power of words. I hope I am able to pass along their gifts to my own son Levi, still working on his first recipes, to whom this book is dedicated.

Notes

1. Ashkenaz refers to the geographical region of Western, Central and Eastern Europe; Sephard has come to designate the Iberian peninsula. Ashkenazi Jews have a wide variety of foodways that privilege the differences in their European regions. The sheer volume of Eastern European Jews who immigrated around the turn of the twentieth century fundamentally shaped contemporary American experiences with Jewish food.
2. For a fascinating study on how corned beef and cabbage became associated with immigrants from Ireland and doughy, white bread became connected to Italian food, see Diner. Barbara Kirschenblatt-Gimblett's beautiful article about Jewish immigrant foodways at the turn of the twentieth century makes the link between such products as Gold Medal Flour and Crisco and their role in "Americanizing" women. For a detailed and surprising investigation into the Maxwell House Haggadah see Balin.
3. Lenny Bruce recorded several different versions of his routine detailing Jewish and non-Jewish behaviors and habits. "Dig. I'm Jewish. . . . Koolaid is *goyish.* All Drake's Cakes are *goyish.* Pumpernickel is Jewish, and, as you know, white bread is very *goyish.* Instant potatoes—goyish. Black cherry soda's very Jewish. Macaroons are *very* Jewish—very Jewish cake. Fruit salad is Jewish. Lime jello is *goyish.* Lime soda is *very goyish.*" See Kaufman (123). Kaufman quotes Cohen (31) and compares it to recorded versions on *Lenny Bruce: Let The Buyer Beware*, disc 3, cut 17 (recorded Oct. 5, 1961) and disc 5, cut 6 (recorded Nov. 1961).
4. Milton Berle has been widely credited with saying, "Anytime someone orders a pastrami on white bread, somewhere a Jew dies." David Sax begins his study of the Jewish American delicatessen with the aphorism attributed to the comedian. As a joke it has a longer history and has been in circulation for at least seventy years. See Popick.
5. See Sue Fishkoff's description of the decision and the required steps in the kashering process in *Kosher Nation* (3–23, 46–71).
6. The editors are grateful to the University of Nebraska Press for allowing this essay to be published in this volume even before it appears in the forthcoming collection *Global Jewish Foodways: A History*, edited by Hasia R. Diner and Simone Cinotto (Univ. of Nebraska, 2018).
7. The editors are grateful to Columbia University Press for allowing this essay to be reprinted from *Religion, Food and Eating in North America*, edited by Benjamin E. Zeller, Marie W. Dallam, Reid L. Neilson, and Nora L. Rubel (Columbia Univ., 2014), pp. 234–49.

Works Cited

Anderson, Jay Allen. "The Study of Contemporary Foodways in American Folklife Research." *Keystone Folklore Quarterly*, vol. 16, 1971, pp. 155–63.

Balin, Carole B. "Good to the Last Drop: The Proliferation of the Maxwell House Haggadah." *My People's Passover Haggadah: What Is the Haggadah Anyway?*, edited by Lawrence A. Hoffman and David Arnow, Jewish Lights, 2008, pp. 85–90.

Barthes, Roland. "Toward a Psychosociology of Contemporary Food Consumption." *Food and Culture: A Reader*, edited by Carole Counihan and Penny Van Esterik, 3rd ed., Routledge, 2013, pp. 23–30.

Brillat-Savarin, Jean Anthelme. *The Physiology of Taste: Or Meditations on Transcendental Gastronomy*. Translated by M. F. K. Fisher, Everyman's Library, 2009. Original translation published 1949; original publication 1825.

Cohen, John, editor. *The Essential Lenny Bruce*. Bell, 1970.

Contois, Emily. "Dunkin' Donuts Coffee: A Site and Source of Bostonian Identity Even during a Lockdown." *Inquisitive Eater*, 22 April 2013, inquisitiveeater.com/2013/04/22/dunkin-donuts-coffee-a-site-and-source-of-bostonian-identity-even-during-a-lockdown/. Accessed 8 Oct. 2017.

Diner, Hasia R. *Hungering for America: Italian, Irish, and Jewish Foodways in the Age of Migration*. Harvard Univ., 2001.

Fishkoff, Sue. *Kosher Nation: Why More and More of America's Food Answers to a Higher Authority*. Schocken, 2010.

Kirschenblatt-Gimblett, Barbara. "Kitchen Judaism." *Getting Comfortable in New York: The American Jewish Home, 1880–1950*, edited by Susan L. Braunstein and Jenna Weissman Joselit, The Jewish Museum, 1990, pp. 76–105.

Kaufman, David. *Jewhooing the Sixties: American Celebrity and Jewish Identity*. Brandeis Univ., 2012, pp. 99–154.

Kuehn, Nancy, Kelly McNamara, Nora M. Khan, and Elizabeth Legris. *Starbucks Coffee Company: Transformation and Renewal*. Harvard Business School Case Study, *Harvard Business Review*, June 2014, pp. 1–71.

Leist, Eric. "25 Social Data Insights on Starbucks and Dunkin Donuts Drinkers." *Social Media Today*, 13 Aug. 2013, www.socialmediatoday.com/content/25-social-data-insights-starbucks-and-dunkin-donuts-drinkers-infographic. Accessed 8 Oct. 2017.

Lenny Bruce: Let the Buyer Beware. Shout! Factory, 5 Oct. 1961, disc 3, cut 17.

———. Shout! Factory, Nov. 1961, disc 5, cut 6.

Lévi-Strauss, Claude. "The Culinary Triangle." *Food and Culture: A Reader*, edited by Carole Counihan and Penny Van Esterik, 3rd ed., Routledge, 2013, pp. 40–47. Originally published 1966.

Meyer, Michael. *The Origin of the Modern Jew: Jewish Identity and European Culture in Germany*, 1749–1824. Wayne State Univ., 1972.

Popick, Barry. "Everytime [*sic*] someone orders a pastrami on white bread, somewhere a Jew dies." *The Big Apple*, 3 Oct. 2015, www.barrypopik.com/index.php/new_york_city/entry/every_time_someone_goes_into_a_deli_and_orders_a_pastrami_on_white_bread. Accessed 8 Oct. 2017.

Simon, Bryant. *Everything but the Coffee: Learning about America from Starbucks*. Univ. of California, 2011.

Weil, Elizabeth. "Who Really Invented the Reuben?" *Saveur*, 6 Sept. 2016, www.saveur.com/reuben-sandwich-origin-history. Accessed 8 Oct. 2017.

Chocolate Migrates to North America with Sephardi Jews

by Deborah R. Prinz

Chocolate is a Jewish immigrant food.

The chocolate trade—including production and consumption—parallels the migrations of Jewish refugees, beginning with Sephardic Jews of Iberian descent in the sixteenth and seventeenth centuries. Indeed, Jews jumped onto the chocolate trail in the early phases of European interaction with the New World drink in diasporic places such as New Spain (now Mexico), Oxford (England), Martinique, Amsterdam, Bayonne (France), Brabant (Belgium), New York and Newport (Rhode Island). It created a path of business interests and appetites that continues in our time. These included chocolate entrepreneurs who fostered, perpetuated, and fed an appetite for the drinking chocolate of the day. In New York, Jewish trade of chocolate may be traced back to 1701. Later, twentieth century Jewish refugees transferred their eating chocolate businesses from one continent to another—such as chocolatiers Eliyahu Fromenchenko of Elite Chocolate, who moved from Latvia to Israel, Karina Chaplinsky of de Karina, who resettled from Argentina to Israel, and Stephen Klein of Bartons, who relocated from Vienna to New York.[1]

Eating chocolate did not exist in New Spain nor did it exist in the British Colonies. In the French Caribbean island of Martinique in the seventeenth century, Benjamin d'Acosta de Andrade, a Jew formerly of Bayonne, cultivated the first cacao trees there. Owner of the two largest sugar plantations, he also established the first cacao-processing plant in French territory. As a result, chocolate eventually became the most important export from Martinique. D'Acosta de Andrade may have been the first to experiment with shaping cacao into pellet form (Bennett). Another early record of eating chocolate comes from 1730 England when Richard Brookes commented that chocolate may be eaten as a solid (Grivetti and Shapiro 913). In 1779, Marquis de Sade, writing from prison to his wife, requested a care package: "The next time you send me a package, please . . . be sure chocolate is included. The cookies must smell like chocolate, as if one were biting into a chocolate bar" (Grivetti and Shapiro 888). Many point to 1847 when Joseph Fry produced bars for eating chocolate in England (Grivetti and Shapiro 878). In 1863 John H. Robertson, a prisoner of the Union Army, wrote about the big supply of chocolate at the commissary and reported that "I ate chocolate candy and drank hot chocolate . . ." (Grivetti and Shapiro 1904).

Sephardi Jews probably engaged with chocolate soon after the first European contact with chocolate, which is said to have occurred during Columbus' fourth voyage (Columbus 232). Certainly that crew included *conversos* (one of several terms for the nuanced Jewish identity of Jews in the period leading up to and following the expulsion of Jews from Spain in 1492 that refer to Jews converted to Christianity and/or descendants of converted Jews). The explorers soon learned that the mysterious looking "almonds" they first saw in the bottom of a canoe were actually cocoa beans used by the indigenous people of the Americas as coinage and as drink. By the end of the sixteenth century, chocolate became quite popular and New Spain (Mexico) exported cocoa beans to Spain. As a result of the kinship and economic ties between Spanish and Portuguese Jews following commercial trade routes, Jews played a significant role, along with Catholic clerics and other traders, in the diffusion of chocolate in the European world (Prinz 3–15).

THE SEPHARDI CHOCOLATE TRAIL

In these early days of European use of chocolate, Spaniards transported it from the New World to the Old World. As Spanish and Portuguese Jews sought refuge from the broad-reaching perils of the Spanish and Portuguese Inquisitions, some packed with them new chocolate tastes, techniques, and opportunities, thereby supplying and extending chocolate to larger markets. Whatever their public or private Jewish practice, Sephardim collaborated with each other to further their business interests. Strong kinship and mercantile ties connected these wanderers along shipping lanes as some became active in the cocoa bean trade and acquired knowledge of chocolate making. The Spanish or Portuguese emigres who escaped west and north in the fifteenth and sixteenth centuries had learned how to source the fermented and dried cocoa beans for trade and import from regions of origin such as Central America, South America, and the Caribbean. They gained the skills for grinding those beans into the chocolate beverages of the day in Spain or New Spain or Recife (Brazil). Along the way, they drank it themselves.

In southwest France, Bayonne's extremely valuable port enabled traders to bypass the Spanish embargoes of 1621 and create lucrative economic traffic with other Jewish communities, particularly in Amsterdam. Bayonne Jews such as Emil Péreire, Isaac Péreire, Alvaro Luiz, Jacome Luiz, and Aaron Colace were crucial merchants in the contraband trade with Spain, including the business of exporting, re-exporting, and smuggling cacao (Israel, *Dutch Primacy* 261; Israel, *Diasporas within Diasporas* 268, 440). Aaron Colace opened a Bayonne office to monitor the market among Spain, Amsterdam, and Caracas, primarily shipping Caracas cocoa beans between Amsterdam and Spain (Piñero 83).[2] In just a six-month period from 1621 to 1622, at least thirty Dutch vessels unloaded goods in Bayonne's port for secret transport to Madrid by mule train through the mountain passes. These ties between the Bayonne Jewish merchants and the Amsterdam Jewish community furthered the commerce of cacao. Because of these chocolate transactions and because of local Sephardi Jewish chocolate makers, Bayonne became known as a chocolate center. Even today, chocolate makers in Bayonne attribute to Jews the distinction of first importing chocolate making to France (Prinz 12).

JEWS IN NEW SPAIN RITUALIZE CHOCOLATE

Jews settled in New Spain (which included Mexico, Central America, Southwest and Central US and Spanish Florida) in the sixteenth century. Records show that by the seventeenth century Jews in New Spain not only took an active role in the cocoa bean trade, they also secreted chocolate into their undercover Jewish ritual life. While chocolate preceded other stimulant drinks of coffee and tea to Europe, it was local to the Americas. In many cases, the resilience of Sephardi immigrants was interwoven with that of the market flexibility of the New World food of chocolate. For Jews attempting to follow Jewish dietary guidelines, the pareve nature of the local chocolate drink, prepared without milk, lent itself to the separation of milk and meat. Chocolate seeped into Jewish customs and celebratory meals for holidays and life-cycle events. Mexican crypto-Jews used chocolate to welcome the Sabbath because wine was scarce in New Spain. Beatriz Enríquez and her sister would not drink their daily chocolate until they had prayed each morning. Chocolate accompanied meals associated with the beginning and end of the fast of Yom Kippur (Day of Atonement). Gaspar Váez broke his 1640 Yom Kippur fast with chocolate, eggs, salad, pies, fish, and olives (Gitlitz and Davidson 103). Isabel de Rivera testified on October 7, 1642, that a year before, on Yom Kippur, Doña Juana, who was married to the wealthy Simón Váez Sevilla, sent "thick chocolate and sweet things made in her house" (Ferry 9). Around 1645 Gabriel de Granada and his family washed down their pre-fast meal with chocolate, having dined on fish, eggs, and vegetables. Others reported that they preceded the Day of Atonement with fruit and chocolate and that they broke the fast with chocolate and similar treats (Gitlitz 364). Beatriz Enríquez, at the age of 22, testified that when her husband left for long business trips, she took advantage of her sadness to hide her abstinence from chocolate and food on *día grande*. From the window she pretended to be crying over the absence of her husband and with this suffering she was able to hide from her *negras* (Negro servants) the fact that she ate nothing and did not drink chocolate that day (Ferry 13).

On fast days, observant Jews refrain from drinking liquids as well as eating any food. On Catholic fast days drinking can be permitted. Cautious lest their non-Jewish servants report them to the Inquisition, Jews in New Spain developed subterfuges not to be caught observing Jewish fast days, including the Day of Atonement. In order not to be seen abstaining from drinking the customary morning chocolate on fast days, Amaro Díaz Martaraña and her husband staged a falling out with each other at the table. When chocolate was brought to them, they pretended to be offended and spilt it on the servants. They separated for the duration of the twenty-five-hour fast and reconciled in the evening when the holy day had ended (Gitlitz 398–99).

Chocolate use extended to sad times as well. Holding vigil for the dying Doña Blanca Méndez de Rivera, her daughters and granddaughters spent a day in reflection and prayer, fortified by a special meal of chocolate and pickled fish brought from Veracruz by the merchant Mathias Rodríguez de Olivera, as Margarita de Rivera recalled for the Inquisition (1644) (Ferry 8–9). The proceedings of the trial of Gabriel de Granada (October 1642) report witness testimony about the period of mourning for a relative. Gabriel sent to her the hard boiled eggs and chocolate which was eaten by the said widow and her children ("Process or Trial" 93). At funerals, the Mexican Váez family (1630s) ate chocolate, raisins, almonds, salad, and homemade bread, but never any meat (Liebman 47, 83, 84; Gitlitz and Davidson 44).

JEWISH CHOCOLATE TRADERS IN NEW SPAIN

Several *conversos* paved the chocolate trade routes in New Spain. In 1641 Manuel Álvarez de Arellano imported goods from Seville and distributed them throughout New Spain. That year, he left for Spain with Mexican chocolate and other items, but he was arrested by Inquisition officials in 1642 and sent to New Spain for trial. Luis Núñez Pérez, a Portuguese *converso* and cacao (cocoa bean) retail merchant in New Spain, was arrested in June 1642, not long after he arrived. A vendor of cocoa beans, he was sentenced to reconciliation with the Catholic Church and life imprisonment at the age of thirty. Pedro de Campos became a successful cacao merchant in Campeche by the 1640s. In 1624 Francisco López de Fonseca, who spent his childhood in Portugal and Spain, sailed to Cartagena at the age of 16 to help his uncle in his general store and then traveled to Venezuela, where he purchased a shipment of cacao and sailed for New Spain. Another Jewish cacao merchant, Duarte Castaño, operating out of Caracas, exchanged cacao for silver and products desired in Venezuela. During one expedition to Veracruz in 1645, he carried twenty-five *fanegas* (dry measure of about 1/2 bushels) of cacao belonging to Rabbi Benito Enríquez, eight *fanegas* sent by Pedro de Campos, as well as his own cargo of one hundred *fanegas*, all on consignment of *converso* Antonio Méndez Chillón. Francisco Franco de Moreira imported and distributed cacao from Venezuela. Manuel López Nuñez controlled the tax on cacao. Luis de Burgos, at age sixty-three or sixty-four, purchased a store that specialized in cacao, chocolate, and sugar. When he was arrested in 1645, his shop was sequestered by the Inquisition. They left its manager, Juan de Acosta, in charge. Even when Burgos was finally released, the Inquisition tribunal kept the store. The Burgos store inventory included cacao that had been sourced from Maracaibo, Venezuela, Guayaquil, Ecuador, and Soconusco, Mexico. Another crypto-Jew and chocolate retailer, Luis Núñez, acquired a chocolate store in 1642 and was shortly thereafter arrested. In the records of the auto-da-fé of March 30, 1648, we learn about a grower of cocoa beans in Zacatula, forty-year-old Melchor Rodríguez

López, who had been born in Portugal and immigrated to Mexico (Hordes, *To the End of the Earth* 42, 53–54, 83–84, 92, 109; Ferry 16–17; Liebman 317, 327).

Antonio Méndez Chillón, one of the wealthiest Jews sought out by the Mexican Inquisition, pursued a very sophisticated cacao trade. He arrived in Mexico from Angola in 1629 and settled in Veracruz, becoming a leading importer of Venezuelan cacao to New Spain. His crypto-Jewish agents and merchants in Gibraltar as well as Caracas and Maracaibo bartered for cacao and monitored the fluctuations in price, quality, and availability of the cacao beans (Ferry 52; Hordes, *Crypto-Jews* 81). Following his arrest, the Inquisition tried to confiscate a load of cacao from his manager, Orozco, but since it had not yet been transmitted into his ownership, the Veracruz *maestre* (master) would not turn it over to the tribunal, though the Inquisition kept trying until 1664. When the Inquisition officials inventoried Méndez Chillón's home after his arrest, they found immense wealth, including 8,486 Mexican silver pesos, 349 gold Spanish doubloons, and trunks of silver, jewelry, tableware, gold, and pearls. Chillón sought to protect his illegitimate children. He hid his seven-year-old daughter at the oldest convent in Mexico City and put a house in Veracruz into her name to secure the payments to the convent. Perhaps because he had not been found to have networked with other crypto-Jews nor observed any Jewish rituals, his imprisonment was shorter than that of others. He was nevertheless deported to Cadiz, Spain, in 1647, and sadly, the Inquisition confiscated the monies he had set aside for his children (Ferry 25ff., 41, 57, 63).

THE FIRST CHOCOLATE IMPORTS NORTH OF MESO-AMERICA

The earliest appearances of chocolate in the area we now know as the United States occurred in a period spanning from the eighth century to the seventeenth century. Chocolate usage initially connects Mesoamericans to the southwest United States where chocolate residue has been identified in shallow clay bowls at an eighth century settlement of the ancestral Pueblo peoples at Alkali Ridge of southeastern Utah. The discovery of chocolate in clay cylinders north of Central Mexico, in Chaco Canyon, New Mexico, dates back to about 1000 CE (D. K. Washburn, W. N. Washburn, and Shipkova; Crown and Hurst 2110–13). Also a manuscript dated September 29, 1641, reports the plight of a ship named the *Nuestra Señora del Rosario y el Carmen* traveling the Bahamas Channel to Spain. Caught in a hurricane, the captain tossed much of the cargo in order to save the ship. However, he elected not to throw the valuable chocolate/cocoa beans overboard. After the storm passed, the ship finally landed at St. Augustine, Florida. *Conversos* were among the settlers of St. Augustine, Florida, since 1565 and may have enjoyed these first tastes of the shipwrecked cocoa (see Cabezon and Grivetti 669–98). In 1670 the city of Boston granted permission to Dorothy Jones and Jane Barnard to open a "Coffee and Chucaletto" house (Gay 281). Finally, British customs records show cocoa arriving in America in 1682: "1682 . . . Jamaica . . . to . . . Boston" (Gay 281).

PRE-REVOLUTIONARY COLONIAL CHOCOLATE MAKING

Since those early imports and coffee houses, coarsely ground drinking chocolate became plentiful and was commonly imbibed as a beverage in the British Colonies of North America. In the North American Colonial period the Sephardi trading network imported and shipped cocoa beans beginning in New York in 1701, based on the first known business record of the Jew Isaac Marquez.[3] Sephardim also manufactured and retailed chocolate; they joined Quakers and others in the chocolate business in colonial America (Prinz 40). American Jewish historian Jacob Rader Marcus has intimated, "Jewish shopkeepers specialized in cocoa and chocolate which they secured in large quantities from their co-religionists in Curaçao. . . . Chocolate in fact may have been a Sephardic Jewish specialty . . ." (*The Colonial American Jew* 673). Indeed, many pioneering Jewish and other chocolate endeavors preceded the beginning of the Baker Chocolate Company, started in 1780, which has billed itself "Baker's Chocolate Brand America's Oldest" (Sammarco; "Baker's Chocolate").

Colonists imported cocoa beans from the Caribbean, Central America or South America for drinking purposes; the beans were retailed at dry good stores. Servants or slaves often performed the laborious tasks of preparing a hot chocolate: first, they tended and roasted the cocoa beans over a fire, then they shelled each bean individually, ground them over a warmed chocolate stone with a roller, and cooled the chocolate into solid balls. The solidified chocolate, wrapped in used newspapers or rags, was often stored randomly, likely absorbing the smells of nearby foodstuffs. Larger fifty-pound chocolate quantities were generally sold in boxes. Some households kept twenty-five to fifty pounds of chocolate on hand, enough to supply a family of four with a customary daily hot chocolate for about a month. Before indulging, the grated hardened chocolate required further mixing with water and sugar using a special stirrer called a *molinillo*, or mill, while heating in the special chocolate pot. The resulting hot chocolate resembled that found elsewhere at that time and today in Mexico and Guatemala. It might have then been served in unique cups especially for the drinking of chocolate. Such specialized tools were available at local dry goods shops, some run by Sephardim and some by Ashkenazim. The proximity to cocoa bean origins kept prices accessible in the Colonies. While some countries such as France established monopolies on chocolate and Britain levied high taxes on it, the Colonies did neither. By contrast, the Colonies supported fifty or more chocolate makers, with approximately twenty-four in Philadelphia by 1776. Surprisingly, America had more chocolate per capita than Europe. Benjamin Franklin sold chocolate in his print shop (Snyder; Gay 289).

COLONIAL CHOCOLATE DRINKING HABITS

Hot chocolate made from cocoa beans, sometimes called "cocoa nuts" or "chocolate nutts," dressed up breakfast or supper. It could have comprised the entire meal. Martha and George Washington served chocolate in addition to coffee and tea at breakfast daily at Mount Vernon (McLeod). Coffeehouses and chocolate houses were as fashionable in the Colonies as they were in England. Ships' crews savored chocolate provisions on board. While the governments of England and Holland sentenced people to hang for stealing one pound of chocolate, it was so reasonably priced in North America that it was dispensed to soldiers, prisoners, and poor people (Gay 285). The pervasiveness of chocolate in the Colonies made its trade particularly advantageous for early Jewish colonists and new immigrants to the continent.

COLONIAL JEWS TRADE, MANUFACTURE AND CONSUME CHOCOLATE

Sephardi Jewish merchants imported, wholesaled and retailed cocoa beans. They also prepared and consumed the beverage in the Colonies. Jews such as Nathan Simson engaged in significant trade of cocoa and shipped more than

33,000 pounds of it between 1710 and 1721. Seven years later, the Jew Rodrigo Pacheco imported 30,000 pounds of cocoa through New York's port, the equivalent of approximately one-third of the total annual import through New York in the late 1760s in the period known as the New York chocolate boom (Oppenheim Collection, 255/18/4; see also Clarence-Smith, *Coffee and Cocoa* and and Clarence-Smith, "Chocolate Consumption").

Jews imported cocoa beans from long distances as well as from colonial ports. The cocoa came primarily from Caracas as well as Curaçao, Jamaica, and Haiti. Rachel Luis imported cocoa beans from Curaçao (Marcus, *The Colonial American Jew* 2:562). Simson secured cocoa beans that had been imported to South Carolina (Marcus, *The Colonial American Jew* 2:625). In 1734, one of Rodrigo Pacheco's ships sailed from New York to Curaçao where it loaded cocoa beans to be exchanged for rice in Charleston. Then it continued on to Falmouth, England (Marcus, *The Colonial American Jew* 2:1494 n. 38).[4] Between 1702 and 1704 Joseph Bueno, who was awarded his license to trade and traffic in New York in 1683, bought large quantities of cocoa beans in Newport (Marcus, *The Colonial American Jew* 2:488 n. 16) and dealt with "24,000 wt (pounds) coko" (Shapiro 58). Bueno shipped cocoa beans to England from Newport, Rhode Island on the sloop *Mary*. In at least one case his captain attempted to circumvent the law. Claiming that his ship leaked, Bueno's captain unloaded in New York and stored the cocoa beans in Bueno's warehouse rather than at the custom shed, purportedly awaiting an increase in the price. Bueno was charged and fined (Hershkowitz, "Some Aspects" 22).[5]

Up and down the Coastline, Sephardi and Ashkenazi Jews traded cocoa beans and sold prepared chocolate. Records indicate that in 1748–49, Sephardi Isaac Navarro in Maryland announced that he ". . . makes and sells as good Chocolate as was ever made in England at 4s.6d per pounds. . . ." In 1773 in Baltimore, Michael Gratz used the Globe Mill to make mustard as well as chocolate (*Paving Our Way*; Marcus, *The Colonial American Jew* 2:1498 n. 15). Others in the retail business included Benjamin Levy, the first Jew to settle permanently in Baltimore, who ran the largest ad in the *Maryland Journal and Advertiser* for his chocolate and snuff business in 1773 (*Paving Our Way*; Marcus, *American Jewry* 350; also, Special Collection 11496). In the 1770s Abraham Wagg, who married Rachel Gomez, daughter of Mordecai and Rebecca on July 4, 1770, engaged in the business of wholesale grocer and chocolate manufacturer (Duker 1–4). Around the same time, Benjamin Lyon and Isaac Werden in Canada competed for business, including their chocolate sales (Marcus, *Early American Jewry* 236). Levy Solomons of Albany opened a chocolate factory to serve his Dutch customers in 1790 ("Items Relating to the Solomons Family" 376). Jacob Philipson advertised chocolate and sugar in the *Missouri Gazette* in 1808 when he announced the opening of his new store (Business Advertisements).

Since the start of the eighteenth century, Jews in North America had been familiar with chocolate, proficient at trading the beans, and able to turn those beans into chocolate. This sample of estate inventories highlights these interests. When these Sephardim died, their estates included quantities of beans, chocolate grinding equipment, and appurtenances for chocolate consumption.

> [1708] Jacob Bueno, NY: One hundred bags of cocoa worth as well as chocolate stones.
>
> [1709] Isaac Pinheiro, NY: Thirty pounds of chocolate, a copper chocolate pot, and ten chocolate pots.
>
> [1725] Abraham de Lucena, NY: One copper chocolate pot.
>
> [1750] Moses Louzada, NY: Four "baggs cocoa."
>
> [1750] Mordecai Gomez, NY: One chocolate pot, sixteen chocolate cups, two boxes of chocolate of fifty pounds each, and six "srunes coco."
>
> [1782] Aaron Lopez, Newport: Fifty pounds of chocolate, eight brown china chocolate bowls, eleven turtle-shell chocolate bowls, and four and a half dozen chocolate and cake pans.[6]

By 1832, chocolate's familiarity in the Jewish community allowed Dr. Daniel L. M. Peixotto to argue during the cholera epidemic that in deference to physical health Jews in New York should not observe the fast day of the ninth of *Av*, *Tishah B'Av*. Rather "they should be permitted to take a light meal of coffee, tea or cocoa with dry toast . . ." (Shapiro 59).

This inexpensive and ubiquitous chocolate business of Colonial North America was also advanced by the cocoa bean trade, chocolate manufacturing, and retail of Sephardi immigrants and cousins Aaron Lopez and the Gomez family members. Each family achieved success in its respective Jewish and non-Jewish communities. These merchant families enjoyed far-ranging, intercolonial and intercontinental chocolate trading businesses. They made their fortunes and exerted their influence based, in part, on their fluency with chocolate making and the related import/export business of chocolate. Using their hemispheric familial ties, various family members imported the raw product and produced the ground chocolate. Their business ties were interwoven with familial matters as when, in 1753, Daniel Gomez wrote from New York to Aaron Lopez in Newport inquiring about the price of cocoa and at the same time notifying Lopez of the death of his wife. Gomez's business with Lopez's father-in-law, Jacob R. Rivera, also included chocolate (Correspondence Daniel Gomez).

THE GOMEZ FAMILY WORKS CHOCOLATE

The multigenerational Gomez gusto for all areas of the chocolate business in New York mingled with that of their Newport cousin through their Sephardi roots, marriage vows, religious ties, and financial interests. Five members of the Gomez family within two generations were involved in the chocolate business of this leading family of the Sephardi and general community of New York. The sizable home of Luis (Lewis) Moses Gomez was taxed at nearly ten times the value of the Jews' rented house of worship, which reveals a sign of his prosperity (Sarna 524, 525). Luis' sons, Mordecai and Daniel, served as Spanish interpreters to the Admiralty and Supreme Courts; Daniel served for some twenty years at this post (Hershkowitz, "Some Aspects" 14). The State Assembly met at Mordecai Gomez's house (Gelles 146 n. 4). At New York's Congregation Shearith Israel the Gomez family enjoyed the most prestigious seats. Isaac bequeathed silver ornaments for the Torah to his eldest son, Mordecai (Gelles 143). Moses Gomez laid the first stone of the new synagogue (Pool 34) and Luis Moses Gomez, along with his son Mordecai, signed the contract with the mason (Pool 40). The affluent Gomez family's donation was the highest from any single family (Pool 36).[7] Of the twenty-five Sephardi *Parnassim* (members of the leadership committee), twenty were part of the Gomez family (D. and T. de Sola Pool 525). Mordecai, Daniel and David, along with father Luis Moses Gomez, appeared in the title for the Jewish cemetery in 1729 (D. de Sola Pool 23, 40). The northwest gallery of the synagogue's women's section, called the *Banco,* was reserved for the Gomez family women.

The Patriarch Luis Moses Gomez was born in Madrid. According to Gomez family tradition his father, Isaac Gomez, a Spanish nobleman and a favorite at court, was warned by the king that the Inquisition was about to arrest him and confiscate his estate. He quickly sent his wife and infant son, Moses, to France to secure their safety along with "money, jewels and plate" (Solis, 140). They arrived in New York around 1696. In 1706, Luis obtained a letter of denization (bestowing some of the privileges of a British subject) which enabled him and his family to live in New York and to purchase land. He became a very successful merchant and a prominent leader of the community (Solis 142).

Gomez family members were among the several Colonial and Revolutionary period North American Jews who engaged in the manufacture, retail and consumption of cocoa and chocolate: Mordecai Gomez (1688–1750), his wife Rebecca (1713–1801), his brother Daniel (1695–1780), Mordecai and Rebecca's son, Moses (1744–1826), and their nephew, Isaac (1768–1831) (Stern 185). Daniel Gomez engaged in a large and lucrative business in New York, trading with the West Indies, Madeira, Barbados, Curacao, London, and Dublin; between 1739 and 1772, he sent 133 ships to Curacao. He corresponded and traded with Sephardi Jews in these locales (Klooster 354). In addition to retailing chocolate, Daniel Gomez imported more than 20,860 pounds cocoa to New York via Curacao between 1728 and 1747 (Daniel Gomez Account Book). In 1759 Gomez advertised boxes of drinking chocolate for sale at the corner of Bruling's Slip in New York City (*New York Gazette or the Weekly Post Boy*). When Mordecai Gomez died in 1750, he left several chocolate accoutrements in his estate inventory including "16 chocolate cupps, whole and broken, 1 chocolate pott; 2 boxes Chocolate 50 lbs each and 6 Surnis (840 pounds) Coco [Surinam]" (L. M. Friedman 75ff.). For many years Moses Gomez earned his living as a chocolate maker. In 1788 he announced his search for his runaway "indented servant" who was "used to chocolate making" (*New Jersey Journal* 4). Moses Gomez and Company also advertised the private sale of "1 ton of Carracas cocoa" (*Mercantile Advertiser*). In 1815 Isaac Gomez's advertisement ran at least forty-three times: "Isaac Gomez Jr. and Co 6 boxes chocolate" (*The National Advocate*).[8]

Although there were a few other contemporaneous female chocolate retailers, Rebecca Gomez was the only woman known to manufacture it. Her business knowledge led her to advertise about her unique chocolate which reflected a growing sophistication about marketing. Using her family reputation and name to good effect, she not only ventured into business but also participated in a trend toward specialization. Rebecca's manufacturing marked shifts in commerce toward industrialization in the decades of the 1770s and 1780s. The youngest child of Abraham Haim Lucena, she married Mordecai Gomez in New York, on May 4, 1741, five years after his first wife died (Gelles

128 n. 8). Rebecca advertised her chocolate business in local New York newspapers in the late 1770s and early 1780s. She plied her quality wholesale and retail chocolate made at the dry goods and "Chocolate Manufactory." For example:

> [1779] Rebecca Gomez at the Chocolate Manufactory
> Corner of Ann and Nassau-Street
> HAS FOR SALE . . .
> Own manufactured Chocolate, warranted free from any sediments and pure.
> Great allowance made to those who buy to sell again.
> (*New York Gazette and Weekly Mercury* [January 25 1779]: 2)

> [1780] Rebecca Gomez
> Has for sale at the CHOCOLATE Manufactory
> No. 14 upper end Nassau-Street between . . .
> SUPERFINE warranted CHOCOLATE, wholesale and retail. . . .
> (*Royal Gazette*)

> [1781] Chocolate
> Manufactured in the best manner, warranted fine and good, to be sold wholesale and retail,
> by REBECCA GOMEZ at the Chocolate Manufactory, No. 57, Nassau Street between Commissary Butler's and the Brick Meeting . . .
> (*New York Gazette and Weekly Mercury* [February 12 1781]: 4)

> [1781] CHOCOLATE
> WARRANTED fine and good, wholesale and retail, at reasonable rates, by REBECCA GOMEZ, at the chocolate manufactory, No. 57, Nassau Street. . . .
> (*New York Gazette and Weekly Mercury* [March 12, 1781]: 4)

Rebecca reflected a late-eighteenth-century interest in chocolate quality, and increased focus on one product, that is, "superfine, free from any sediments and pure. . . ." Her advertising savvy reflected a growing sophistication about marketing. Her advertisements leave off information about how she ground the chocolate, by hand or by mill, by herself or with employees. Upon her own death, at nearly eighty years of age, Rebecca left a bequest to Congregation Shearith Israel (Hershkowitz, "Wills of Early New York Jews"; L. M. Friedman 75).

Only in 2015 did Gomez family descendants learn of their family's multi-generational immersion into the chocolate business of the colonial period of North America. The hundreds, maybe even thousands, of Gomez family members today no longer work in the chocolate business. Robert Jacobs, one of those descendants, says however: "Everyone in the family loves chocolate" (Jacobs) and they have a favorite chocolate frosted cake (see recipe). Jacobs now chairs the Gomez Foundation for Mill House, the oldest extant Jewish structure in the United States, the fur trading outpost that was run by Luis' sons, listed on the National Register of Historic Places. Jacobs now realizes that his family's love for chocolate has deep historical authenticity.

AARON LOPEZ: CHOCOLATE IN RHODE ISLAND

By the middle of the 1770s Aaron Lopez was the highest taxpayer in Newport and the richest man there (Chyet, *A Merchant of Eminence* 191). His trading ventures and volume put him on par with the Browns of Providence, benefactors of Brown University (Marcus, *Colonial American Jew* 2:642), and transformed Newport into the second largest mercantile port after New York ("Aaron Lopez Papers"). He became the first Jew to be naturalized in Massachusetts by establishing residency there. Claiming overpopulation, Rhode Island did not grant him naturalization. Until 1765, Lopez's trade moved mostly coastwise among Boston, New York, Philadelphia and Charleston. He expanded across the Atlantic, importing from Bristol, England to satisfy the American desire for British and European products and to avoid London prices (Chyet, *Lopez of Newport* 83ff.). By 1767, Lopez had sent at least nine vessels to the West Indian trade ports, shipping livestock, poultry, pickled oysters, candles, naval stores, bricks, lumber, and even silverware; return cargoes brought cocoa beans, molasses, rum, coffee, and sugar (Marcus, *Colonial American Jew* 2:649). In 1768, he ran thirty-seven coastal voyages (Marcus, *Colonial American Jew* 2:628). By the time of the Revolution, he had financial interests in nearly thirty of the one hundred sailing vessels associated with Newport and the Triangular Trade, especially remarkable for a newcomer.

From his British wall-papered, wood-timbered office overlooking the port of Newport, Gomez cousin, immigrant Aaron Lopez, used labeled pigeon holes in the rafters to monitor his many vessels and related businesses which included chocolate (Bigelow 2:4). He imported cocoa beans, hired people to grind the cocoa beans into chocolate, sold that chocolate, and exported chocolate. Lopez's chocolate business differed from that of the Gomez family in that he neither advertised nor focused on quality. Despite those choices, he too became quite wealthy and a leader of the Jewish community.

Born in 1731 in Portugal, and known then as Duarte, he and his family lived publicly as Christians and secretly as Jews. Lopez escaped Portugal to live a full Jewish life. He arrived in Newport where his older half-brother, Moses, was already living and set up shop in 1750. Among other enterprises he used the current technology of spermaceti, extracting wax from whale oil for candle making, an improvement over wax candles. In 1763, Aaron married the daughter of Jacob Rodriguez Rivera, another Newport Sephardi merchant. Even with all of the demands of his business, Lopez maintained his Sabbath observance. He "rigidly observed . . . Saturday as holy time" and closed his business from Friday afternoon to Monday morning. Over a three year period none of his ships left port on a Saturday. He laid the cornerstone for the new Newport synagogue, the Touro Synagogue. He customarily ended his letters with: "Sabbath is coming on fast" (Sarna 527).

Lopez also used chocolate in Jewish contexts. The reasonably-priced chocolate made its way into *tzedakah* gifts which Lopez distributed on behalf of the Jewish community and synagogue. In March 1765 he organized ". . . *sedakah* . . . delivered [to] Mrs. Lazarus towards her support 14 pounds of rice, a pound of tea and 2 pounds of chocolate" (Aaron Lopez 667_March, 1765). ". . . Sedakah Sunries for Judah Abrahams . . . " fitting him out for Surinam with "28 pounds of bread, an iron pot, a pound of tea, two pounds of chocolate . . ." (Aaron Lopez 667_20 April 1770). Also, Lopez records may be the first to connect chocolate with Passover. In April 1772, Lopez paid Joseph Pinto for "6 lb Chocolate for Pesah (Passover)" (Aaron Lopez 736_14 April 1772).

The chocolate that Lopez secured was ground and made ready for consumption through other people, whose wages offered some opportunity for economic security. Those who worked for Lopez included his co-religionist Joseph Pinto (Marcus, *Colonial American Jew* 2:673). His account books note other workers as "Negroes."[9] He also hired "Negro chocolate grinders" Prince Updike, Cornelius Casey, and Abraham Casey,[10] paying them four to five shillings per pound of ground chocolate.[11] These men were probably freed slaves or possibly worked to purchase their freedom as was customary in Newport.[12] Between December 1770 and August 1771, Joseph Pinto paid off his debts for purchases of clothes and food by grinding chocolate. In 1770, Lopez' notebook indicates that Pinto's servant or slave named Cezsar ground cocoa beans in twenty-five, fifty, and one hundred pound amounts (Lopez Memorandum Book 459/491; Lopez Memorandum Book R/118/318; Lopez Memorandum

Book 716/327). The quantities suggest that the stone method of grinding by hand was primarily used.

Captains and agents represented Lopez in many of his endeavors; they sold chocolate on his behalf, paid off accounts in cocoa beans, and bought chocolate from others. He also retailed chocolate at his dry goods shop on Thames Street in Newport. His primarily non-Jewish customers bought chocolate there every few months in small quantities of about one or two pounds at the cost of about two pounds sterling (MS 231 Folder 1/9 AJA). Lopez also bought for his personal use. After the Revolution, Samuel Wallis of Boston received from Mr. Ezekiel for the account of Mr. Aaron Lopez "five boxes of Chocolate weighing 110 pounds, 110 pounds, 110 pounds, 102 pounds, and 108 pounds totaling 540 pounds . . . forty pounds of Chocolate over to fill the Boxes" (Chyet, *Lopez of Newport* 28).[13]

The Revolution caused Lopez significant business losses. Ever a patriot, he stopped importing tea at the time of the Boston Tea Party. As the local paper reported, "Mr. Aaron Lopez, owner of the ship, *Jacob*, . . . has assured us in writing that said ship has not India TEA on board and that he thinks himself happy in giving such assurance" (*Essex Gazette* 94). In 1779, he described the wartime hardships of the inhabitants of Leicester and Newport to a Captain Anthony, noting that they lacked basic food. Jews in particular suffered due to a scarcity of kosher food. They had not tasted any meat, but once in two months. Fish was not to be had, and they were forced to subsist on chocolate and coffee (Chyet, *Lopez of Newport* 160).[14]

Jacob Rader Marcus was quite correct in calling chocolate a "Sephardic Jewish specialty." Sephardim immigrated to New Spain and added to its chocolate culture. In the Colonies the chocolate of Sephardim contributed to the growth and sustenance of the nascent Jewish American community. These seventeenth and eighteenth-century Jewish merchants dipped deeply into the chocolate concerns of their day. They benefited from trading cocoa beans, enjoyed the personal consumption of the chocolate beverage, and profited from it as a commodity. As chocolate journeyed with Sephardi exiles, it continued to grow in popularity. Overall, these Jews engaged with the commercial interests and technological advances in chocolate of the day, which contributed to the pioneering cocoa and chocolate enterprises of Colonial Period of North America and to the historic chocolate of New Spain. Out of necessity Sephardi Jews sought refuge in distant locales yet stayed in touch through trade; chocolate played a crucial role in deepening those ties and providing these refugees opportunities for success in New Spain and in the Colonies.

* * * * * *

Recipe: Colonial Period Hot Chocolate

[1796]

Take six Pounds of cocoa-nuts, one of anise-seeds, four ounces of long pepper, one of cinnamon, a quarter of a pound of almonds, one ounce of pistachios, as much achiote as will make it the colour of brick, three grains of musk, and as much ambergris, six pounds of loaf-sugar, one ounce of nutmegs, dry and beat them, and searce [sift] them through a fine sieve; your almonds must be beat to a paste and mixed with the other ingredients; then dip your sugar in orange-flower or rose water, and put it in a skillet on a very gentle charcoal fire; then put in the spice and stew it well together, then the musk and ambergris, then put in the cocoa-nuts last of all, then achiote, wetting it with the water the sugar was dipt in; stew all these very well together over a hotter fire than before; then take it up and put it into boxes, or what form you like, and set it to dry in a warm place: the pistachios and almonds must be a little beat in a mortar, then ground on a stone. (Glasse 341)

Recipe: Chocolate Pudding (actually a cake; this recipe is updated)

Ingredients:

1 cup milk or dark chocolate, crumbled
1 cup graham cracker crumbs or grated crackers
1 cup sugar
5 eggs separated

Instructions:

Preheat the oven to 375°F. Lightly grease an 8-inch springform pan. Melt the chocolate in a large heatproof bowl set over a pan of simmering water; remove from the heat to cool. Beat together the egg yolks and sugar. In a separate bowl, beat the egg whites. Fold the egg yolks and sugar into the cooled chocolate. Fold in the graham cracker crumbs. Fold the egg whites into the chocolate mix. Pour the batter into the prepared pan. Bake for 30 minutes. Cool in the pan. To serve, cut into wedges.
Quantity: 6–8 servings. (Levy 94)[15]

Recipe: Gomez "Family Cake"

When the Gomez descendants gather, they enjoy a delicious chocolate iced cake dubbed "family cake."

For best results, make sure your ingredients—eggs, butter and milk—are at room temperature except where indicated.

Ingredients:

For the cake
4 large eggs, separated
2 sticks sweet (unsalted) butter
1 cup sugar
1 cup whole milk
2½ cups cake flour
2½ teaspoons baking powder
1 teaspoon salt
1 teaspoon vanilla

For the icing
1 pound dark chocolate (preferably 8 ounces bittersweet and 8 ounces 70% dark chocolate)
½–¾ stick of salted butter
½ cup cold milk (more if mixture is too thick)
A bit of sugar to taste

1) Preheat oven to 375° F.

2) Grease (butter) and flour 3 round 8-inch cake pans.

3) Separate eggs and set aside.

4) Sift flour together with baking powder and salt. Set aside.

5) Cream butter and sugar in bowl (use electric mixture or hand held beaters). Add egg yolks one at a time. Beat well.

6) Alternately add small amounts of flour mixture and milk to the butter mixture. When the last of the flour is added, beat in vanilla.

7) In separate bowl, beat egg whites until very stiff. Using a large spoon or rubber spatula, gently fold egg whites into batter. Mix gently but thoroughly.

8) Pour mixture into prepared cake pans. Bake for about 15 minutes, until a tester comes out clean. Be careful not to over bake. Cake should be very moist.

9) To prepare the icing: Melt chocolate and butter in a double boiler or bain marie (do not microwave).

Add about ½ cup of milk. Mix well. Cool slightly, but spread while still warm. Spread icing between layers, on top and on sides of cake.

Notes

1. This article is adapted from Deborah R. Prinz, *On the Chocolate Trail: A Delicious Adventure Connecting Jews, Religions, History, Travel, Rituals and Recipes to the Magic of Cacao*. For further materials about chocolate in the British colonies, see the bonus materials for *On the Chocolate Trail* at onthechocolatetrail.org.
2. A Jamaican Jew, Isaac Nunes, had contact with a brother living in Bayonne (Fortune 133).
3. He imported twenty-five pounds. Marquez was endenizened in New York, October 16, 1695 and made a Freeman on September 17, 1697. Denization extended some rights, such as owning land, to foreigners under British law. When naturalization developed denization fell out of use (see Stern 185; Liber 30). He died in New York in 1706. Customs records in the decade following 1701 list merchant cargoes of mainly "cocoa, rum, wine, fur, and fabrics." The customs records for cargoes in New York include cocoa beans for the decade after 1715 (see Hershkowitz, "Some Aspects" 25).
4. He also traded to Jamaica, through New York, Lisbon, Genoa, and Barcelona.
5. Another court case concerning cocoa arose when Moses Levy sued Nathan Simson and Jacob Franks, executors of Samuel Levy's estate, claiming that Samuel Levy had sold him spoiled cocoa with salt in it in 1722.
6. Prinz 52; Hershkowitz, "Original Inventories" 283, 300–01, 307-08, 318-19, 409, 419, 425, 440-42; Aaron Lopez Estate Inventory, 1783, Judicial Archives, Boston, MA.
7. Luis Moses Gomez also contributed the highest gift from a Jewish community member to rebuilding the Trinity Church steeple (D. de Sola Pool 39).
8. By this time it was not unusual for merchants to place advertisements.
9. According to Keith Stokes of the Newport Chamber of Commerce in an email message to the author, September, 2009: "Enslaved Africans and Mulattos (African & Indian mix) comprised nearly 20 percent of entire Newport population by 1770. For the most part, slaves were trained to work within urban seaport economies, i.e., sail lofts, rope works, fish processing, rum making and spermaceti candles, etc. Many of these slaves were apprenticed and trained as artisans. Slaves in the households of Lopez, Rivera, and other Newport Jews were given Jewish names including Sara, Moses, Rebecca, etc. These close work, home and religious relationships would create unique bonds between master and slave. When a five-year-old enslaved African boy drowned in Newport Harbor, Aaron Lopez funded the proper burial and marker. By 1780, the Free African Union Society was formed at Newport, a first of its kind in the Americas where former slaves organized and chartered a self-help organization with the Rhode Island General Assembly."
10. The *Memorandum Book O #554* makes it clear that Prince worked for the Updike family. For further information about Prince Updike, see *Spinner's Book* #715/36.

11. June 16, 1773, John Baker of Boston charged James Baker 1 pound 2 shillings 6 pence for "one days work at your Chocolate Mill." Miller "Calendar" (5).
12. For nearly a century, 1725–1807, the American slave trade was virtually synonymous with that of Rhode Island. Rhode Island merchants controlled between sixty and eighty percent of the American slave traffic. However, according to Bert Lippincott, Librarian and Genealogist, Newport Historical Society, only one percent of Lopez's trade dealt in slaves (interview). See S. S. Friedman (121).
13. For example, Joseph and William Rotch of Nantucket reported to Aaron Lopez about the coffee, chocolate, molasses, and rum they had sold on his account in December of 1780.
14. On a voyage from London which began in May of 1750, George Fisher described that because of the small allotment of food allowed by the captain, "myself and most of my family subsisted almost entirely on Coffee, Tea and chocolate, wherewith we were well provided. . . ." See Taliaferro.
15. This is the first known American Jewish cookbook.

Works Cited

Aaron Lopez 667_March, 1765. Newport Historical Society, Newport, RI.

Aaron Lopez 667_20 April 1770. Newport Historical Society, Newport, RI.

Aaron Lopez 736_14 April 1772. Newport Historical Society, Newport, RI.

Aaron Lopez Estate Inventory, Death Notices, 1783, MS 231/1/4, AJA, Cincinnati, OH.

"Aaron Lopez Papers." Rhode Island Historical Society, www.rihs.org/mssinv/Mss541.htm. Accessed 25 April 2017.

"Baker's Chocolate." *Kraft*, brands.kraftfoods.com/BakersChocolate/heritage.htm. Accessed August 2009.

Bennett, Ralph G. "The Sephardic Path to North America." Www.sefarad.org/publication/lm/030/bennett.html. Accessed 2006.

Bigelow, Bruce Macmillan. "*The Commerce of Rhode Island with The West Indies Before the American Revolution,* Parts 1 and 2." Dissertation, Brown Univ., 1930.

Business Advertisements from the *Missouri Gazette* 1808, American Jewish Archives, Cincinnati, OH.

Cabezon, Beatriz, and Louis Evan Grivetti. "Paleography and the St. Augustine Chocolate Saga." *Chocolate: History, Culture and Heritage*, edited by Louis Evan Grivetti and Howard-Yana Shapiro, Wiley, 2009, pp. 669–98.

Chyet, Stanley F. "*A Merchant of Eminence: The Story of Aaron Lopez.*" Dissertation, Hebrew Union College–Jewish Institute of Religion, 1960.

———. *Lopez of Newport.* Wayne State Univ., 1970.

Clarence-Smith, William G. "Chocolate Consumption from the Sixteenth Century to the Great Chocolate Boom." *The Economics of Chocolate*, edited by Mara P. Squicciarini and Johan Swinnen, Oxford Univ., 2016, pp. 43–70.

———. *Coffee and Cocoa, 1765–1915.* Routledge, 2000.

Columbus, Ferdinand. *The Life of Admiral Christopher Columbus*, www.americainclass.org/wp-content/uploads/2013/09/4-Christopher-Columbus.pdf. Accessed 15 July 2017.

Crown, Patricia L., and W. Jeffrey Hurst. "Evidence of Cacao Use in the Prehispanic American Southwest," *Proceedings of the National Academy of Sciences*, vol. 106, no. 7, Feb. 2009, pp. 2110–13, www.pnas.org/content/106/7/2110.full.pdf, doi:10.1073/pnas.0812817106. Accessed 2 March 2017.

Daniel Gomez Account Book, Microfilm 597, AJA, Cincinnati, OH.

Duker, Abraham G. "Emerging Culture Patterns in American Jewish Life: The Psycho-Social Approach to the Study of Jewish Life in America." *Publications of the American Jewish Historical Society*, vol. 39, Sept. 1949–June 1950, pp. 1–4.

Essex Gazette. 11 Jan. 1774, p. 94.

Ferry, Robert J. "Trading Cacao: A View from Veracruz: 1629–1645." *Nuevo Mundo Mundos Neuvos*, 2006, nuevomundo.revues.org/1430, p. 9. Accessed Nov. 2011.

Fortune, Stephen Alexander. *Merchants and Jews: The Struggle for British West Indian Commerce 1650–1750*. Center for Latin American Studies Book, Univ. of Florida, 1984.

Friedman, Lee M. *Early American Jews.* Harvard, 1934.

Friedman, Saul S. *Jews and the American Slave Trade.* Transaction, 1998.

Gay, James. "Chocolate Production and Uses in 17th and 18th Century North America." *Chocolate: History, Culture and Heritage*, edited by Louis Evan Grivetti and Howard-Yana Shapiro, Wiley, 2009, pp. 281–300.

Gelles, Edith B., editor. *The Letters of Abigail Franks 1733–1748.* Yale Univ., 2004.

Gitlitz, David. *Secrecy and Deceit: The Religion of the Crypto-Jews.* Jewish Publication Society; Univ. of New Mexico, 1996.

Gitlitz, David, and Linda Kay Davidson. *A Drizzle of Honey: The Lives and Recipes of Spain's Secret Jews.* St. Martin's Griffin, 1999.

Glasse, Hannah. *The Art of Cookery Made Plain and Easy, 1796 Edition.* United States Historical Research Service, 1994.

Correspondence Daniel Gomez to Aaron Lopez, Microfilm 597, New York, 19 June 1753, American Jewish Archives (AJA), Cincinnati, OH.

Grivetti, Louis Evan, and Howard-Yana Shapiro. "Chocolate Timeline." *Chocolate: History, Culture and Heritage*, edited by Louis Evan Grivetti and Howard-Yana Shapiro, Wiley, 2009, pp. 855–928.

Hershkowitz, Leo. "Original Inventories of Early American Jews (1682–1763)." *American Jewish History*, vol. 90, no. 3, Sept. 2002, pp. 239–321.

———. "Some Aspects of the New York Jewish Merchant and Community, 1654–1820." *American Jewish Historical Quarterly, vol.* 66, nos. 1–4, Sept. 1976–June 1977, pp. 10–34.

———. "Wills of Early New York Jews (1743–1774) Part II." *American Jewish Historical Quarterly*, vol. 56, nos. 1–4, Sept. 1966–June 1967, np.

Hordes, Stanley M. *Crypto-Jews of New Mexico.* Columbia Univ., 2005.

———. *To the End of the Earth: A History of the Crypto-Jews of New Mexico.* Columbia Univ., 2005.

Israel, Jonathan Irvine. *Diasporas within Diasporas: Jews, Crypto-Jews and the World Maritime Empires (1540–1740).* Brill, 2002.

———. *Dutch Primacy in World Trade 1585–1740.* Clarendon, 1989.

"Items Relating to the Solomons Family, New York." *Publications of the American Jewish Historical Society*, vol. 27, 1920, pp. 376–78.

Jacobs, Robert. Personal interview. 9 Nov. 2015.

Klooster, Willem. "Jews in Suriname and Curaçao." *The Jews and the Expansion of Europe to the West, 1450 to 1800,* edited by Paulo Bernardini and Norman Fiering, Berghahn, 2004, pp. 350–68.

Levy, Esther. *The Jewish Cookery Book, on Principles of Economy, adapted for Jewish Housekeepers with the addition of many useful medicinal recipes and other valuable information related to housekeeping and domestic management.* Turner, 1871.

Liber 30 of Conveyances Registers Office Borough of Manhattan, New York City, An Account of his Majesty's Revenue of the Province of New York, P255/Box#19, American Jewish Historical Society (AJHS), New York City, New York.

Liebman, Seymour B. *The Jews in New Spain: Faith, Flame and Inquisition.* Univ. of Miami, 1970.

Lippincott, Bert. Librarian and Genealogist, Newport Historical Society. Personal interview. 10 Sept. 2009.

Lopez Memorandum Book 459/491. Newport Historical Society, Newport, RI.

Lopez Memorandum Book R/118/318. Newport Historical Society, Newport, RI.

Lopez Memorandum Book 716/327. Newport Historical Society, Newport, RI.

Marcus, Jacob Rader. *American Jewry: Documents Eighteenth Century.* Hebrew Union College, 1959.

———. *The Colonial American Jew, 1492–1776.* Wayne State Univ., 1970.

———. *Early American Jewry: The Jews of New York, England and Canada 1649–1794.* Jewish Publication Society, 1951.

McLeod, Stephen A. *Dining with the Washingtons: Historic Recipes, Entertainment and Hospitality from Mount Vernon.* Univ. of North Carolina, 2011.

Memorandum Book O #554. Lopez Collection, Newport Historical Society, Newport, RI, p. 119.

Mercantile Advertiser. 20 July 1799.

———. 1 Aug. 1799.

MS 231 Folder 1/9 AJA, Cincinnati, OH; Lopez Letterbook 640, 21 Feb., 1781, p. 66 Newport Historical Society, Newport, Rhode Island.

The National Advocate. 15 March 1815–26 June 1815.

New Jersey Journal. 3, 17, 19, 24 Sept. 1788, p. 4.

New York Gazette and Weekly Mercury. 25 Jan. 1779, p. 2.

———. 12 Feb. 1781, p. 4.

———. 12 March 1781, p. 4.

New York Gazette or the Weekly Post Boy. 5, 12 Feb. 1759. Oppenheim Collection, Daniel Gomez file/Box 4, AJHS, New York.

Oppenheim Collection, 255/18/4. American Jewish Historical Society, New York, NY.

Paving Our Way: Early Maryland Jewish Life 1632–1845: A Living History Resource Kit, presented by the Jewish Museum of Maryland, www.jhsm.org/html/documents/PavingOurWay1.3.07.pdf. Accessed 2006.

Piñero, Eugenio. "The Cacao Economy of the Eighteenth-Century Province of Caracas and the Spanish Cacao Market." *The Hispanic American Historical Review,* vol. 68, no. 1, Feb. 1988, pp. 75–100.

Pool, David de Sola. "The Mill Street Synagogue (1730–1817) of the Congregation Shearith Israel (New York)." 1930 pamphlet at AJHS, New York.

Pool, David de Sola, and Tamar de Sola Pool. *An Old Faith in the New World: Portrait of Shearith Israel 1654–1954.* Columbia Univ., 1955.

Prinz, Deborah R. *On the Chocolate Trail: A Delicious Adventure Connecting Jews, Religions, History, Travel, Rituals and Recipes to the Magic of Cacao.* Jewish Lights, 2012.

"Process or Trial of Gabriel de Granada, Mexico 1642." *Publication of the American Jewish Historical Society*, vol. 7, 1899, pp. 1–127.

Royal Gazette. 2 Dec. 1780, p. 3.

Sammarco, Anthony M. *The Baker Chocolate Factory: A Sweet History*. History, 2009.

Sarna, Jonathan. "Jews in British America." *The Jews and the Expansion of Europe to the West, 1450 to 1800*, edited by Paulo Bernardini and Norman Fiering, Berghahn, 2015, pp. 519–31.

Shapiro, Celia D. "Nation of Nowhere: Jewish Role in Colonial American Chocolate." *Chocolate: History, Culture and Heritage*, edited by Louis Evan Grivetti and Howard-Yana Shapiro, Wiley, 2009, pp. 49–64.

Snyder, Rodney. "History of Chocolate: Chocolate in the American Colonies." *Colonial Williamsburg*, www.history.org/history/teaching/enewsletter/volume9/jan11/featurearticle.cfm. Accessed Nov. 2011.

Solis, Elvira N. "Note on Isaac Gomez and Lewis Moses Gomez from an Old Family Record." *Publications of the American Jewish Historical Society Journal*, vol. 11, 1903, pp. 139–44.

Special Collection 11496, AJA, Cincinnati, OH.

Spinner's Book #715/36. Newport Historical Society, Newport, RI.

Stern, Malcolm. *First American Jewish Families 600 Genealogies 1654–1977*. American Jewish Archives and American Jewish Historical Society, 1978.

Stokes, Keith. Newport Chamber of Commerce. Email message to author, Sept. 2009.

Taliaferro, John "The Ranger." "The Fisher Story." *Geni*, ch. XXIII, www.geni.com/people/John-The-Ranger-Taliaferro/6000000000350946881. Accessed 17 Sept. 2017.

Washburn, Dorothy K., William N. Washburn, and Petia A. Shipkova. "Cacao Consumption During the 8th century at Alkali Ridge, Southeastern Utah." *Journal of Archaeological Science*, vol. 40, no. 4, 2013, 2007–13.

Global Jewish Peddling and the Matter of Food*

by Hasia Diner

Historians and other writers who have contemplated the experience of Jews in the American West in the nineteenth century have repeatedly told a story, one which they believed said much about the idea of Jews in strange places. The story, unverifiable, although its appearance in a number of memoirs gives it an air of authenticity, tells the tale of a Jewish peddler. A young man, like millions of his peers, joined in the great migration of the Jewish people, a movement which changed the profile of world Jewry. Like so many of the men, he decided that his chances for economic success depended upon his willingness to put a pack on his back, and head out to the hinterlands to sell consumer goods to customers with limited access to the market place. He, like they, went anywhere and everywhere that people in need of material goods welcomed the arrival into their home of someone willing to bring it. Most began their careers selling by foot, graduating eventually to an animal-drawn wagon. Wherever they went they depended directly on the good-will of their customers to buy the items which they carried, and also to lodge them at night and to feed them.

In this narrative, one which has entered into the realm of American Jewish folklore, the peddler, a regular itinerant merchant who sold among the Cherokee Indians in Oklahoma, had been offered something to eat by his hospitable customers. Despite his hunger and after his long hours on the road, he refused to partake of the food offered to him by his customers. The food violated the Jewish dietary laws. It consisted of forbidden ingredients and had been prepared in vessels tainted by the *treife,* or impure, foods that had been cooked in them. But he did accept one item. He consumed an egg cooked in its shell. The egg conformed to the rules of *kashrut* and the fact that it had never directly touched an unkosher pot, protected as it was by its hard shell, the Jewish peddler could consume it. So commonly did this act of eating take place, that the story, repeated in works of history and memoir, in jokes and in theatrical renditions, went on to declare that some of the Cherokee therefore referred to all Jews, regardless of occupation or levels of religious observance, as "egg eaters" (Marks 53).

This small anecdote, whether true or not, contains within it a universe of meaning in terms of the history of Jewish migrations, Jewish occupations, Judaism as a religious system, and the role of food. In the long nineteenth century, from the end of the eighteenth into the early twentieth, millions of Jews left their places of long-term residence—Europe, the Ottoman Empire and North Africa—and set out to a variety of new lands. Those lands stretched from the Americas to southern Africa to Oceania, taking Jews mostly to the United States but also Cuba, Mexico, Peru, South Africa, and Australia, as well as to regions of Europe like Ireland, Sweden, Wales, and Scotland, which had never had a Jewish population before.

They left for a combination of mainly economic reasons but also in order to address their anomalous status in the Christian and Muslim lands where Jews had lived for centuries. Their economic motivations reflected both crises in the lands they had lived in and the opening up of new opportunities in the lands to which they went. Most of those prospects, born of the age of colonialism, European expansion, and the spread of consumer capitalism, involved commerce. As a broad generalization, the period of Jewish on-the-road peddling in the New World coincided with the rise of new economic realities, which put small amounts of cash in the hands of people who had previously lived without it. With that cash, these women and men could buy items that they had never had before. They could afford to augment their material lives with a variety of consumer goods that either had not existed before or which the better-off and urban people had enjoyed. Such items as eyeglasses and bed linens, pictures and picture frames, buttons, needles, thread, tablecloths, could be had by ever-expanding populations of customers, in remote places, and the Jewish immigrant men who took to the road and served as the middlemen between these neophyte consumers and the stuff produced in the cities.

The massive transfer of Jewish people, a migration of over four million throughout the nineteenth century, pivoted around peddling, an occupation that Jews knew, and which reflected internal credit networks. While each of the places from which Jews left and each of the places to which they went had a separate and unique history, young men willing to peddle made up the majority of those who went, and certainly in the earlier stages of the migration. For example, the majority of Jewish men who migrated to Lithuania at the end of the nineteenth century started out as peddlers, known there as "weekly men." The bulk of Macedonian Jews, men mostly from the town of Monastir, who went to the Amazon region, began their New World careers as peddlers. So too the Bavarian Jews—all males, who fanned out across the United States in the 1830s and 1840s—got launched through peddling (for a fuller discussion, see Diner).

The history of Jewish migration cannot be disassociated from the history of peddling, and the history of Jewish peddling cannot be understood without the matter of food. Peddlers, these Jewish men who in the main hailed from traditional backgrounds, had to negotiate food as they set off on their roads, and as a concern it shaped how they related to their customers and also how it bound them to the Jews who already lived in these places and provided the new peddlers with goods and credit.

PRE-MIGRATION JEWISH FOOD

Food vexed and challenged the millions of Jewish men on the roads of the New World in ways that it had not in their long history of peddling that had taken place before the great migration. Extending backward into the Middle Ages and encompassing nearly the entire world, as known at the time, Jews engaged in the retail sale of wares from packs on their backs or from animal-driven carts. They sold to Jews and non-Jews. Both Jewish women and men developed their routes, forged relationships with customers, helped stimulate desire for new goods, and served as fixtures of many local economies. In some regions and towns peddlers outnumbered nonpeddlers in the Jewish community, and the clustering of Jews in this one occupational group affected nearly all aspects of the Jewish experience.

Numbers varied from place to place and changed over time. They also could be elusive in that the peddlers came in and out of towns and regions, and many individuals peddled at some point or another in their lifetimes. But just a few samplings of efforts at counting peddlers in premigration Europe demonstrate the significance of peddling to Jewish history. In 1863 one writer for the

French Jewish newspaper, *L'Univers Israelit* remarked, looking backward to an earlier era, that "during the First Empire peddling was the chief occupation of Jews. Thus according to the census of 1808, twenty of approximately twenty-six Jewish families of Fontainebleu were so engaged: in Versailles, Orleans and Nantes all the Jews were peddlers." In Württemberg in 1812, no fewer than 85.5 percent of the Jews made a living as "hucksters," and a study of Polish Jewry in the nineteenth century stated quite simply, "A majority of the Jewish population in Poland made their living in trade, but this principally meant peddled trade rather than retail." It may not be at all outrageous to suggest that every European Jew would have known peddlers, as family members, neighbors, and real presences in the ordinary course of everyday life (quoted in Szajkowski 307; Landes 13; Orla-Bukowska 94).

Notably, Jewish peddling in Europe had been different, vis-à-vis its practice and its relationship to food. Jewish communities in the premodern and premigration settings, for example, made certain that either individual Jews or the community as a whole provided food and lodging for the Jewish peddlers. Fulfilling the fundamental religious obligation of *hachnassat orchim,* or the welcoming of visitors, took on particular salience in an environment where vast numbers of Jews walked the roads selling goods and found themselves in need of places to eat and sleep.

The existence of hundreds of scattered Jewish communities, in relative proximity to each other, also meant that these peddlers in the Germanic states, Poland, Alsace, and elsewhere on the continent, as well in the vast stretches of the Ottoman Empire, did not have to return home every week for the Sabbath. Since they could avail themselves of Sabbath services, and Sabbath food in the towns along their route, they could traverse large regions and return home just a few times a year. They spent the weekly Sabbath and the many Jewish holidays away from their own families but still basked in the comfort of Jewish homes, resting, praying, and consuming the food items associated with the holy days. In fact Old World Jewish peddling exposed relatively humble Jews to the foodways of Jews in towns and regions beyond their familiar ones.

But even on ordinary days, the Jews who sold goods along the roads of the premigration world had to deal with the issue of food. For the most part these poor and generally traditional men maintained the dietary laws. They had to eat kosher food, and geographic and demographic patterns made that possible. As they plied their routes, they could depend upon Jews in the small towns to feed them and know that the food that they put in their bodies conformed to the strictures of *halakhah,* Jewish law.

Particularly in some of the most important places from which Jewish peddlers left—Bavaria, Alsace, Lithuania—most Jews lived in small enclaves, scattered throughout the countryside. The existence of these little clusters meant that the Jewish peddler could always avail himself of the obligatory hospitality of the community by which the peddlers would be fed and lodged and as such be dependent neither on their own wits nor on their non-Jewish customers. The string of small communities, the nodes of Jewish life along their routes, meant that *kashrut* did not have to be negotiated, compromised, violated, or, if observed, done so with great effort and difficulty. The ability of pre-migration Jewish peddlers to adhere to their dietary code benefitted also from the close relationship which existed between Jews and non-Jews, neighbors for centuries.

In the European and Ottoman settings, Jewish peddling played a crucial role in forging relationships between Jews and non-Jews, and these relationships existed in environments where Jews had lived for centuries. Non-Jews, whether French or German speakers, Polish, Lithuanian, Hungarian, Czech, or Arabic, knew Jews, after long eras of exposure. Jewish peddlers and their non-Jewish customers spoke the same languages, and evidence exists that the customers in many places incorporated Jewish words, particularly Yiddish, Ladino, and Judeao-Arabic, into their own lexicons as they interacted with the Jewish peddlers. Jews had been in their midst for so long that the non-Jews, Christian or Muslim, knew the intricacies of the Jewish calendar and, importantly here, they knew what Jews ate and what they could not. We learn from a variety of sources that at times Jewish peddlers did spend the night in Christian homes or in inns catering to many different kinds of wayfarers. The Jewish peddlers, as it were, taught their Christian customers something about Judaism.

Given the ubiquity of the Jewish peddlers and the familiarity non-Jews had with Jewish customs, inn keepers, non-Jews, allowed Jewish peddlers to store their cooking pots at the inns. The Jewish peddlers often impressed their marks on their own utensils so that they could be kept safely and away from contamination from non-kosher foodstuffs. Every time they returned to that establishment, they had access to the cooking vessels and could prepare food for themselves. In a family reminiscence of the peddling experience in the early nineteenth century, in Rhenbischofsheim, a small town in Germany, Moses Kahnmann's grandson recalled his grandfather describing how he "occasionally might find in a village inn or with a friendly peasant a pan especially marked with the sign of *kashrut*, for the exclusive use of Jewish guests," the majority of whom came as peddlers. Others, both in personal memoirs and in historical studies, observed that "the pedlars stayed overnight with peasant acquaintances with whom they left their own kosher crockery for repeated uses." Peasant meant non-Jew, and such respectful behaviors demonstrated the possibility of Jewish-Christian amity in an otherwise hostile environment and underscored the significance of the peddlers as historical actors (Cahman 112–14, 121).[1]

In the largest sense, despite all of the many difficulties and hostility they faced from the non-Jews, particularly state officials who set up onerous restrictions on where the Jews could go and imposed steep taxes on them, as well as the poverty which most endured, they did not have to worry about food.

PEDDLING AND MIGRATION

The act of leave-taking pivoted in a number of ways around the peddling phenomenon. Notably, these New World Jewish peddlers may not themselves have ever peddled before their migrations. So many came from the ranks of young men unable to find a place for themselves in the local economies of the regions where they had grown up. Migration offered them a way of establishing themselves as adults. They may themselves have been too young to have ever peddled themselves, but when they needed to find a means of migration and a means of making a living in their new homes, they turned to what they knew. After all, they would have known in their immediate families and in their villages many peddlers whose experiences and skills the potential migrant drew upon. In addition, these young Jewish emigrants abandoned precisely those places where intense competition from other Jews in the field of peddling had made it impossible for them, as young people, to get started with their lives. Finally, the young men poised to emigrate by taking up the peddlers' pack, departed from towns and regions that no longer needed peddlers because new commercial realities undercut the peddlers'—and the Jews'—longstanding modes of making a living.

Instead these young men began a process of moving outward, discovering as Jews a number of new worlds, and peddling, the old familiar economic *modus operandi* of the Jews, structured that linked physical movement and the process of discovery. This new age of Jewish peddling took Jews out of continental Europe and brought them over the course of the next two-and-a-half centuries to no fewer spots around the globe than the British Isles, the Americas—North, South, and Central—South Africa, and Australia.[2]

In each one of these places, and the many specific regions within them, peddlers as the first Jews, and sometimes the first white people, penetrated these unknown spaces. In various lands the activities of the peddlers cleared the ground for the eventual formation of settled Jewish communities, while in others the peddlers—and the Jewish presence—disappeared leaving few traces.

The history of Jewish peddling in each new location has a history of its own. Each one stands as worthy of analysis. Jewish peddling in South and Central America followed a particular course no doubt different than that of Jewish peddling in South Africa or Canada. Furthermore, within any one of these continents or countries, local variations also made for many different histories of Jewish peddling and Jewish migration. For example, Jewish peddlers in Quebec, who sold to French-speaking Catholic customers who evinced hostility towards the idea of Canada as a modern, liberal, and British-oriented nation, had a particular set of experiences that diverged from those of Jewish peddlers who cast their lot in the Anglophone provinces—where Protestantism predominated and most women and men embraced their connections to Great Britain and its economic and political practices. Likewise, in South Africa, Jewish peddlers sold at one time or another to the Afrikaner Boers and British, as well as to Native customers, who had been colonized by both previously-named groups. Each constituency had a different set of reactions to the peddlers as Jews, immigrants primarily from Lithuania, and bearers of consumer goods. Each history needs to be explored and each stands on its own. Young Jewish men who showed up in the American South to peddle their wares found a particular racial landscape, one in which the black-white divide created a set of social practices not replicated in New England or upstate New York, where differences of class rather than color structured political relationships, which the peddlers had to know about and deal with. Further west, the presence of Indians and Mexicans as customers forced Jewish peddlers fresh from Posen or Lithuania to confront yet another set of on-the-ground realities as they sought to accomplish the goals of the migration: earn money, settle down, marry, or bring wives and children left behind in either Europe or some other large city, and get on with life.

Yet certain characteristics have been shared by all New World Jewish peddling histories, regardless of continent or country, and food made an appearance as an issue in all of these places. First, unlike Old World peddling, the immigrant peddlers sold only to non-Jews. This perhaps obvious point had tremendous historical significance, not just for the peddlers themselves but for the development of Jewish communities in these places. The young Jewish man who decided to leave Alsace or Lithuania—two important senders of Jewish migrant-peddlers—and try his luck in the Mississippi Delta, the Pacific Northwest, as well as the Transvaal, the Australian outback, the Argentine Pampas, the Irish midlands, the mining regions of Wales, or the foothills of the Andes, had no string of Jewish enclaves to turn to when the day ended, when the sun set on Friday, or when Jewish holidays punctuated the calendar.

These peddlers spent the days of the week only among non-Jews, depending upon their customers for a place to sleep and eat before setting out again on the road. Since Jewish peddlers divided up the countryside among themselves, no one encroaching upon another's territory, they lived pretty much devoid of contact with other Jews. This reality reflected the fact that the first of the peddlers, as pioneers, went to places where no Jew had been before. Those who immigrated later and entered the field took the place of the Jewish peddlers who had amassed enough savings to be able to own their shops in town. While the later peddlers sold to non-Jews who had already had become acquainted with Jews, they still did not share the road or their weekday time with other Jews, and the newcomer peddlers, like their predecessors, spent days on end with no other Jews around them. After all, they spent the entire week, save the Sabbath, with non-Jews who had never had contact with Jews before.

This then meant that New World Jewish peddlers, unlike their counterparts in the Old World, did not travel as far and chose to organize their selling lives in such a way as to be able to get back to Jewish enclaves for the Sabbath. The life histories of many of these immigrant peddlers repeatedly noted that their lives marched according to a kind of weekly rhythm. They went out on their routes on Sundays and returned by Friday to whatever existed in the way of a Jewish hub for the Sabbath where they encountered Jewish food, fellowship, and rest.

Joseph Jacob in his 1919 apologetic defense of the Jewish people, *The Jewish Contribution to Civilization*, described how in England—which in terms of Jewish migration history must be thought of as a "new world"—"it was customary for the Jews of the seaport towns . . . to send out their sons every Monday morning to neighboring villages as hawkers, who would return in time for the Friday night meal." These hawkers, the British word of choice for peddler, came to be known within the Jewish community as "Wochers," that is, "weekly people" (219). In Ireland, to which several thousand Lithuanian Jews emigrated after the 1880s and where nearly all the men peddled at one time or another,

Jews described themselves and were described by their customers as "weekly men," the ones who showed up week after week at the farmhouse doors, ready to collect payment for previously purchased goods and to show the woman of the home some new "things" to buy.[3] Throughout Spanish-speaking South and Central America, local people referred to the Jewish peddlers, whether Ashkenazim from Europe or Sephardim from the Ottoman Empire as "semananiks," that is, weeklies. In Mississippi, as in many Southern Jewish communities, former peddlers, turned shopkeepers, provided the space for those still on the road needing a Sabbath resting place. In Natchez, the Millstein's house became the place where, "many of the peddlers who came home . . . after a week's work would gather . . . for the Sabbath" (L. E. Turitz and E. Turitz 26). Simon Wolf recalled that "twenty or thirty Jewish peddlers," gathered at his mid-nineteenth century home in Uhrichsville, Ohio every Sabbath and that his aunt provided them with food during their weekly sojourns off the road (quoted in Panitz 19).

In other places around the Jewish peddlers' New World, Jewish women opened up boarding houses, which served the men during the weekends when they came back to town. In the towns, the peddlers not only got their chance to rest and eat home-cooked meals, prepared by Jewish women, but they also transacted business. Here they paid back the wholesalers from whom they had gotten their goods and then filled up their packs so that they could go back out onto the road.

Notably, many of the small towns to which the peddlers went on the weekend themselves lacked facilities for kosher food. They had no ritual slaughterers, for example, and as such the peddlers who came for the Sabbath could not always get the kind of food that before migration would have been the norm. The story of Abraham Kohn, a pious young man, provides a case in point. Despite his commitment to Judaism, a theme which runs through his superb diary written in the 1840s, he spent a year peddling in western Massachusetts and then pursued the same occupation in Illinois. By the middle of that decade he had opened a store in frontier Chicago and joined together with a group of other Jewish men, all Bavarian Jews, who either had peddled, or still did so, in the founding of the village's first Jewish congregation and its first cemetery. In those early Chicago years they lived without access to kosher food. That is, these men, all of whom had spent some amount of time peddling in America, once settled down began to create the infrastructure of Jewish life. But they did not have kosher food. Only five years later, after the founding of the synagogue, when Kohn's more observant mother, Delia, arrived from Bavaria and refused to eat anything other than vegetables, did a kosher slaughterer get brought to Chicago, and it became possible to eat kosher food (Meites 114–16).

For Jews, particularly those who ventured out to places with no Jews, this ubiquitous weekly cycle elevated food to a serious matter, as they had to figure out how to organize their time and even more so, had to decide on their own if the dietary laws mattered or not. It should be kept in mind that most of the Jewish immigrants of this era, male or female, came from traditional homes and communities, and while it is not possible to say with certainty whether all of them had formerly observed the law in a punctilious manner, these migrations, for the most part, began just at the onset of modernization and before the Jews embarked on a process of rethinking what the dietary system meant and why they did not have to follow it. That is, the typical immigrant Jewish peddler, regardless of where he had come from, had before migration lived a life based on this system which divided the world into the ritually edible and inedible. *Kashrut* had enveloped their lives. It had required a communal structure to supervise, certify, and make possible eating the acceptable.

It required trust and a system to enforce it that did not exist in the New World to which they entered. Rather, as nonspeakers of the dominant language, newly arrived peddlers received detailed instructions as to how to begin their careers on the road. The seasoned Jews of Cuba, Chile, Canada, Ireland, Ohio, Alabama—wherever—would write out in Yiddish characters a variety of stock phrases for the newcomer. Among them they included variants on the question: "May I lodge in your home?"

The memoirs we have, the scraps of information which detail the day-to-day lives of the peddlers, point to a range of strategies to deal with the food problem.

Certainly some did not fret the details of *kashrut*. They ate what they could, and may not have worried about it at all, but given the class level of most of the peddlers, it is reasonable to assume that most came from fairly traditional backgrounds and were relatively unaffected by the secularization of the Jews going on in the cities of Europe. As such their journeys on the road and into the kitchens of their customers likely offered their first encounters with "treife" and the first challenges to their own standards of observance, something that was—premigration—relatively unselfconscious, based on customary and familiar behavior and not ideology.

These first encounters may have played a role in loosening the bonds that tied Jews in the New World to the formal and structural constraints of Judaism. Here they found themselves in new, alien, and utterly "un-Jewish" places, which forced them, or possibly allowed some, to decide for themselves what they wanted to do as Jews.

That is, living by themselves amid non-Jews, five days out of seven, forced them to decide on their own what to eat, and what not to eat, what constituted an obligation positively embraced or a burden which the past had imposed upon them and which they now could loosen. Either way, the decision to eat or not eat, like so many other details of Jewish life and law, now lay in their hands. Distances in time and space meant that no one could supervise what they ate.

This led, for many, to create a new reality for observing *kashrut*. During the week, while out on the road, they would eat what they wanted or what they could find. On the weekend, however, when they returned to the nearest Jewish communities—where they paid back their creditors, replenished their packs, and rested—they also got the chance to eat among other Jews, and this often meant that they could eat kosher.

As such it is clear that some of these peddlers observed what we might call situational *kashrut*. That is, during the week as they walked the road, or rode on their horse-drawn wagons, they ate whatever came their way. If their customer who provided lodging and fare offered pork, then they ate pork; if they offered squirrel or other animals that had been hunted, they ate that. But on the weekends, when the peddlers got off the road and "rested," spending Friday night through Sunday in some kind of Jewish setting, they did eat those foods for which both tastes and modes of preparation were familiar and acceptable. Thus Monday through Friday was anything; Friday through Sunday was kosher.

Accounts of peddler-customer interactions also depict how the customers asked the peddlers about their lives back home, places they may never have heard of, like Lithuania or Alsace or Bohemia. One peddler memoir from Georgia retold how Mr. Bedford, an American farmer, questioned Mr. Yampolsky about himself and his life. Besides asking Yampolsky to write out his name, since Bedford had never heard it before, he asked the peddler "Where did [you] come from? . . . What kind of country? . . . What kind of city?"

Mr. Bedford had yet another question to ask, one which got asked nearly everywhere around the peddler's globe. He wanted to know, "What was [Yampolsky's] religion? . . . Why didn't Jews believe in Jesus Christ?" The fact of the Jews' Jewishness surfaced repeatedly. As a matter of discussion it often began over the matter of food. The wife who had allowed the peddler to sleep over, or her husband, oftentimes then invited the peddler to eat with them as well. For the peddler this proved to be no simple matter. While some peddlers in their narratives admitted that after a day on the road, lugging a huge backpack, they would willingly eat anything, even if they preferred to observe the dietary laws. Some peddlers stated categorically that they did not care about those strictures, the system of *kashrut,* and did not have to justify to themselves their violation.

But most of the peddlers, that small minority whose thoughts have been recorded in some form or another, felt compelled to announce to their generous hosts that they could not eat the food. From the point of view of the customers, certainly the first time they had a Jewish peddler in their home, this seemed astounding. Why would anyone turn down pork or ham or whatever food the family put on its table? This then led them to ask the peddler why he would not eat the food that everyone else in the family would consume, and he had to answer basically that his religion would not allow it. Housewives, who seemed to have liked accommodating the peddlers, would then set aside a pot for the peddler's use whenever he came. A memoir of Jewish peddling in New Zealand told the story of a peddler who in 1863 came to a small town and faced a breakfast of ham and eggs. The peddler, eager for a sale but averse to eating the forbidden food, had to figure out a way to do nothing that seemed impolite but yet refrain from consuming the food on the plate in front of him. When his hostess left the room, "he threw [the unkosher food] into the fire. In an instant it blazed and set fire in the chimney and there was great consternation." Unfortunately the memoirist did not describe his hosts' reaction to the fire or if he had to confess what he had done (Davis 18).

As reported by the memoirs, rather than being offended by the peddlers' unwillingness to eat their foods, in most instances families respected the Jews' religious integrity. Certainly in the United States, the most important peddler destination, a strong strain of religiosity pervaded civic life. Since the 1830s and the famous visit to the United States of Alexis de Tocqueville, observers have noted that Americans view religion as a benign force that promotes virtue. At least as embodied in the memoirs of the peddlers and in some of the customers, the Jews' observance of the dictates of their religion won kudos from the Americans. Rather than finding fault with Judaism as a religion that had rejected Jesus and his divinity, the peddlers' customers found the practice of Judaism in their homes something positively good. The father of Leon Schwarz came to peddle in Alabama in the post-Civil War period and on one occasion, according to family lore, he "sat down to eat in a farm house and was served pot-liquor, fried bacon and some greens served with side meat." The elder Schwarz, either because he did not care or was just very hungry "pitched in and ate heartily." His hostess, surprised at Schwarz's willingness to consume all the forbidden food interrogated him. "Mr. Schwarz, I am surprised to see you eat pork. I thought Moses ordered the Jews not to eat any hog meat." As the story went, the peddler surveying the table and seeing nothing but pork, replied, "Ah, madam, if Moses had travelled through Perry County, Alabama, he would never have issued such an order" (Peck 106).

Most immigrant peddlers seem, however, to have gone to great lengths to adhere to the restrictions. They ate only what they could carry in their packs. They supplemented with vegetables, fruits, and the like that they knew to fit the dictates of the system. The memoirs detail the ways in which the peddlers attempted to observe *kashrut* as best they could. Never particularly well educated or knowledgeable Judaically, they believed that they knew what was demanded of them and they did what they could to adhere to a standard that seemed to them "natural" and inherent to their Jewishness. Memoirs abound with narratives of peddlers who, at fortunate times, had a favorite customer with whom they could lodge on a weekly basis, staying every Monday with the same family, every Tuesday, and so on. That customer, and most of the customers were in fact women, designated a special pot for the peddler to use. Either she cooked his acceptable foods for him in that pot, or he, the peddler, did that cooking himself.

This fairly mundane fact offers an interesting window into the potential significance of peddling for the history of Jewish integration. A customer, in Cuba, in Ireland, in Quebec and the Maritime Provinces of Canada, in the American South or West or New England, in South Africa, wherever they might be, developed a relationship, based on the transaction of commerce, with a Jewish peddler and that peddler stayed over one night every week on his route, known in the Jewish peddlers' lexicon as his *medinah*, or kingdom.

Why, the customers asked, can you not eat the same food that we are eating? Why can you, the peddler, not share from the pot, the dishes, or the cutlery that the family is using? This question, repeated in English, French, Spanish, Mayan, Afrikaans, and Cherokee, forced the peddler to say something about the nature of Judaism. Judaism, they would have to say in their stumbling version of those same languages, does not allow us to eat pork, squirrel, rabbit, or the flesh of other forbidden animals. It does not allow us to eat meat that has not been slaughtered in a very particular way, with particular equipment. We cannot consume meat and dairy products at the same time and in less than a set number of hours apart. Our religion does not let us eat food that has been prepared in pots and off plates that may once have had forbidden foods on them, and the like.

Such answers, so fundamental to the Jewish system and so familiar to the non-Jewish customers of the Old World, must on the surface and at first blush have seemed utterly absurd to people whose religion did not require them to eschew particular foods, did not define the universe of food stuffs into the forbidden and the acceptable, from a religious point of view. They would certainly know these categories from an aesthetic or cultural perspective, but not from the point of view of religious truth.

What the peddlers did, then, by explaining what they could or could not eat, involved explicating the laws of *kashrut,* and in the process the nature of Judaism. The peddler, through his food practices, served as a kind of interpreter of Judaism to people who never before had known any Jews. He exposed his customers to the inner life of a religious tradition which they did not know, or if they knew it, they knew it only as something from the pages of the Hebrew Bible and not as something lived by real people.

In the matter of food, the peddler helped shape the process of Jewish integration into all the various destination lands of the great Jewish migration of the long nineteenth century. In all of these places, Jewish men came to enjoy right away or over time a thick bundle of rights, equal to those of the other white men. Having slept in their customers' homes, having eaten at their tables, or having explained to their customers why they would not share their customers' foods, opened the door to familiarity and common citizenship.

Additionally, the fact that Jewish peddlers decided on their own, each man on his own terms, how to handle the food problem tells us something about the kinds of Judaisms which emerged in these new places, the most significant of which—the United States—became the breeding ground for religious innovation. The Judaic system does not give much room to individual negotiation, to individuals deciding what to do, or how and when to do it. It gives them a "set table." Yet our New World immigrant Jewish peddlers when on the road, and off, considered themselves both obliged and able to rethink the nature of Jewish practice. What, they asked themselves, was essential? To what degree did living as a Jew require observing the dietary laws in a meticulous fashion? How important was not sitting down and eating with a non-Jew? Eating from their pots? Sharing their food?

If in the months and years on the road, peddlers, each on his own, decided that it was acceptable to, at times, or in fact all the time, compromise with *kashrut*, then what got eaten became a matter of choice not obligation.

Time on the road peddling in strange new lands empowered them to tinker with tradition, and each individual behaved as he saw fit. His decisions involved a high degree of personal choice and each one, by himself, had to go beyond the commandments as laid out in normative texts inherited from the past. Personal choice and the ability of individuals to mold Judaism as they saw fit became hallmarks, surely, of American Judaism. And we can see, too, how the peddling experience, as it was played out in the realm of food, helped pave the way for a series of religious innovations that characterized the kind of religious life which emerging among Jews in the United States, the single largest receiver of Jewish immigrants, with peddlers accounting for so many.

The history of every Jewish population center in the New World, including the United States, Canada, England and the rest of the British Isles, South Africa, Australia, Mexico, Argentina, and elsewhere in South and Central America, cannot be disassociated from the global history of peddling. Common themes, common processes, and common concerns linked these places and made the history of any one place not all that different from the basic contours of another.

These universals or commonalities connected the experience of being a Jewish peddler at the tip of the Cape of Good Hope with the experience of being a Jewish peddler in, say, Newfoundland, or the tip of Cape Horn with that of Alaska. Yet local stories of Jewish migration and Jewish peddling also deserve to be told in order to enrich and complicate modern Jewish history. In each place the local contours of attitudes towards consumption, allocations of power, distribution of resources, basic religious, ethnic, and racial cleavages in the society, as well as ideas about foreigners, shaped the ways in which Jewish peddlers as immigrants and Jewish immigrants as peddlers made their way.

The long nineteenth century witnessed a Jewish migration of transformative impact, changing the face of world Jewry. Peddling spearheaded that migration, paving the way for the Jewish penetration into so many new lands and regions. Peddling, the experience of being out on the road, day in and day out, made food a central concern for the young immigrant Jewish men who willingly went out on to so many roads, taking them far away from places where they could get kosher food. Without their willingness to go and to negotiate food, the migrations would not have happened. Food functioned as a powerful element in this history as both a matter of personal crisis and choice.

Notes

*. Excerpted from *Global Jewish Foodways: A History*, edited by Hasia R. Diner and Simone Cinotto, by permission of the University of Nebraska Press. Forthcoming Spring 2018.

1. For other references see, Kossover (182). One of the best sources on Alsatian Jewish peddling is Stauben, which originally had been published in the *Revue des deux Mondes* in the late 1850s.
2. For the purposes of thinking about Jewish migration and peddling from the end of the eighteenth century onward, the Netherlands, despite being continental European, functioned as a new world setting. From the beginning of the eighteenth century German, Bohemian, and Polish Jews came to the Netherlands to hawk their goods in towns, many of which did not allow Jews to reside there. Referred to as *smous*, a somewhat pejorative term, Ashkenazi Jews invoked the ire of merchants in Leiden and a number of other cities for their ability to sell goods door-to-door at low prices. For Jewish migrant peddling in the Netherlands, see Israel (114), Kaplan (117), Fuks-Mansfeld, "Enlightenment" (167), and Fuks-Mansfeld, "Arduous Adaptation" (227).
3. On Jewish peddling in Ireland and the use of the term "weekly men" see Hyman (160–66).

Works Cited

Blom, J. C. H., and J. J. Cahen. "Jewish Netherlanders, Netherland Jews, and Jews in the Netherlands, 1870–1940." Blom, Fuks-Mansfled, and Schöffer, pp. 230–96.

Blom, J. C. H., R. G. Fuks-Mansfled, and I. Schöffer. *The History of the Jews in the Netherlands.* Litman Library of Jewish Civilization, 2002.

Cahman, Walter J. "Village and Small-Town Jews in Germany, A Typological Study." *Yearbook of the Leo Baeck Institute*, vol. 19, 1974, pp. 107–30.

Davis, Eliot R. *A Link With the Past.* Unity, 1948.

Diner, Hasia R. *Roads Taken: The Great Jewish Migration to the New World and the Peddlers Who Forged the Way.* Yale Univ., 2015.

Fuks-Mansfield, R. G. "Arduous Adaptation, 1814–1870." Blom, Fuks-Mansfled, and Schöffer, pp. 192–229.

———. "Enlightenment and Emancipation, from c. 1750–1814." Blom, Fuks-Mansfled, and Schöffer, pp. 164–85.

Hyman, Louis. *The Jews of Ireland: From Earliest Times to the Year 1910.* Jewish Historical Society of England, 1972.

Israel, J. "The Republic of the United Netherlands until about 1750: Demography and Economic Activity." Blom, Fuks-Mansfled, and Schöffer, pp. 85–115.

Jacob, Joseph. *Jewish Contributions to Civilization.* Jewish Publication Society, 1919.

Kaplan, Y. "The Jews in the Republic until about 1750: Religious, Cultural and Social Life." Blom, Fuks-Mansfled, and Schöffer, pp. 116–63.

Kossover, Mordecai. "Inland Trade among Polish Jews in the 16th–17th Centuries." *YIVO Bleter*, vol. 15, no. 3, March–April 1940, p. 182.

Landes, David S. "The Jewish Merchant: Typology and Stereotypology in Germany." *Yearbook Leon Baeck Institute*, vol. 19, 1974, pp. 11–23.

Marks, Mel. *Jews Among Indians: Tales of Adventure and Conflict in the Old West.* Benison, 1992.

Meites, Hyman. *History of the Jews of Chicago.* Chicago Jewish Historical Society, 1924.

Orla-Bukowska, Anna Maria. "Shtetl Communities: Another Image." *Polin*, vol. 8, 1994, pp. 89–113.

Panitz, Esther. *Simon Wolf: Private Conscience and Public Image.* Farleigh-Dickinson Univ., 1987.

Peck, Abraham. "That Other 'Peculiar Institution': Jews and Judaism in the Nineteenth Century South." *Modern Judaism*, vol. 7, no. 1, Feb. 1987, pp. 99–114.

Stauben, Daniel. *Scenes of Jewish Life in Alsace.* Joseph Simon, 1979. Orig. pub. in the *Revue des deux Mondes*, late 1850s.

Szajkowski, Zosa. "Growth of the Jewish Population in France (Concluded)." *Jewish Social Studies*, vol. 8, no. 4, 1946, pp. 297–318.

Turitz, Leo E., and Evelyn Turitz. *Jews in Early Mississippi.* Univ. of Mississippi, 1983.

A Younger World: Vegetarian Writing and Recipes in Yiddish as Political Strategies*

by Eve Jochnowitz

Oh, the world will grow younger
And life will be easier
And every complainer will become a singer
It will happen soon, my brothers.[1]

—Morris Winchevsky

The words of "The Future" (*Di Tsukunft*), a poem written by Morris Winchevsky in 1919, imagine a world better in every possible way. Winchevsky's vibrant and expansive vision was representative of the views of countless Jewish activists across any number of ideologies in his time, before the devastation of the Second World War made this kind of optimism forever impossible.

Among the Yiddish speakers in the United States before the Second World War, as in the old country, Socialism, Anarchism, Zionism, and Aguda (an Orthodox political movement founded as a reaction against the other contemporary revolutionary Jewish movements) offered wide-ranging visions of a better future that Jews might bring about for themselves. For many, radical politics were accompanied, or even completely overshadowed, by radical changes in diet. The availability of industrial food alleviated some concerns about bacterial and septic contamination in the food supply while raising other concerns about the nature of food and the role of big business.[2] Economic and agricultural crises led to widespread fear that food might not be reliably available and, in fact, nurses and social workers noted the effects of hunger on health, energy, and recovery times from illness and injury on poor people, many newly poor in the Depression years (Ziegelman and Coe 73; see also Poppendieck). In his second inaugural address, President Roosevelt estimated that one third of the nation was ill-nourished. Changing roles of women and innovations in kitchen technology remade family meals and mealtimes (Jochnowitz, "Feasting on the Future"). Some Jews, seeking to hasten a kinder, more rational, or healthier future, found a cause in vegetarianism.[3] Contemporary journalists and satirists found in vegetarians and vegetarianism endless material for ridicule.

Vegetarian practice calls for deliberate avoidance of animal foods. Normative Jewish practice, which forbids the combination of meat and dairy foods, offers, in the dishes of the dairy repertoire, a built-in meatless (though not fishless) cuisine for Jewish vegetarians to adopt and adapt. While arguments have been made that the roots of Jewish vegetarianism are in Jewish Scripture (see, for instance, Rendsburg; Schwartz; Green), and while Jewish individuals may have followed a vegetarian diet (Schwartz 171–77), the Jewish vegetarian movements in Europe and the Americas are largely modern phenomena rooted in the optimism, and also in the crises and upheavals, of the early twentieth century. These primarily secular vegetarian movements are new; they are informed by the advances of early twentieth-century technology and also beholden to the naiveté of the same period.

Different vegetarians have differing practices regarding liminal foods such as fish, eggs and milk products. The Jewish vegetarian sources in Yiddish cited here from the early twentieth century all reject fish, but use eggs and dairy products, sometimes quite lavishly. Authors from the first half of the century follow the assumption that vegetarianism includes eggs and milk but excludes fish, and do not feel any need to remark on this. Later writers address the differing branches of vegetarianism inspired by veganism, macrobiotics, and ayurvedic cooking. Writing in 1991, Malky Eisenberger, the author the cookbooks *Maykholim tsum gezunt* and *Food for Health*, comments that most vegetarians are comfortable eating eggs, adding "After all, eggs are not animal protein; it is just the egg" (Jochnowitz, "Health, Revolution and a *Yidisher Tam*" 56; Eisenberger; *Food for Health Cookbook*). The diversity of practices among vegetarians, and the fact that many adopted and discarded various stringencies over the years, paired with Alter Kacyzne's assertion that "vegetarianism is a private thing" (5–6)[4] all make it difficult to estimate how many Jews in the early twentieth century practiced vegetarianism, considered themselves vegetarians, or both. When the movement was at its peak in the 1930s, certainly there must have been tens of thousands of Jews who were vegetarians of some sort.

Figure 1: Nayes Folshtendiges Kokhbukh Fir di Yidishe Kikhe, *Vienna, 1854*

The first printed cookbook published in Yiddish of which I am aware is *Nayes folshtendiges kokhbukh fir di yidishe kikhe* published in Vienna in 1854 (fig. 1).[5] This anonymous volume was inward-looking, emphasizing the religious obligations of the Jewish homemaker, and provided detailed instructions for kashering meat and the ritual separation of a small portion of dough from one's bread. The text in the book (though not the title page) was printed in the semi-cursive *vaybertaytsh* typeface that had been used for devotional women's literature in earlier centuries, but was falling out of use by the nineteenth century (Harshav). Oyzer Bloshteyn's much larger *Kokhbukh far Yidishe Froyen*, published in Vilna in 1896, was outward-looking. Bloshteyn collected and translated 668 recipes from cookbooks published in German and other languages to expand and enrich the repertoire of the Jewish homemaker.[6] Vegetarian cookbooks published in Yiddish provided recipes to guide homemakers who explored a new diet or simply wanted to add vegetarian dishes to their culinary repertoire. They also presented arguments for adopting a vegetarian diet and might even include inspiring poems and helpful hints for running a household. As Barbara Kirshenblatt-Gimblett has noted, cookbooks published in the late nineteenth and early twentieth centuries in Yiddish for an immigrant community are about fixing people as well as fixing food:

> Attempts to change the Jewish diet, whether to make it more elegant, more adherent to *kashrut*, more scientific, more American, or less bourgeois, took a variety of forms in the Yiddish cookbooks published in America. Some authors condemned Old World cuisine and promulgated Anglo-American cooking in its stead, others promoted vegetarianism. (Kirshenblatt-Gimblett, "Kitchen Judaism" 86)

Indeed, all of these improvements to the Jewish diet concerned the writers of Yiddish vegetarian treatises and cookbooks. Varied and sometimes contradictory ideologies led the authors to the conclusion of promoting a vegetarian diet.

YIDDISH VEGETARIAN IDEOLOGIES

Figure 2: Lo Tirtsah, *New York, 1899*

לא תרצח

שוחט השור מכה איש
(ישעיה ס״ו 8).

איין אבהאנדלונג איבער „וועגעטאריאניזם“.

איבערזעצט פאן זיין ווערק אין ענגליש

— פון —

א. ה. פריינקעל.

AUTHOR OF

"THOU SHALT NOT KILL" — a treatise on vegetarianism,

"IN GOLD WE TRUST" — a tale of the Ghetto, etc.

— BY —

A. H. FRANKEL.

פרייז 10 סענט

פערלאג פון

ב. ראבינאוויטץ,

398. גרענד סטריט, ניו יארק

Copyrighted 1899 by A. H. Frankel.

All right reserved.

The 1899 book *Lo Tirtsah* (*Thou Shalt not Kill*) by Aaron Frankel (fig. 2) lays out a heartfelt plea for vegetarianism based, as the title makes plain, on resistance to killing.[7] Arguments for a kinder and simpler life are illustrated with quotes from Hebrew scripture and the Jewish liturgy. The author predicts that a peaceful vegetarian world will only come about after dreadful cataclysm. While the book contains no recipes, Frankel does comment in the closing chapter "[a] person of today's world cannot live on raisins and almonds. A many-layered kugel cannot satisfy a modern character" (book 4, p. 94). Frankel's view owes more to traditional religious culture than to the modern political and religious ideologies then gaining ground in the Jewish world, but while many Christian reformers of the late nineteenth century found justification for vegetarianism in scripture, Frankel is a minority within a minority among Jewish vegetarians.

Figure 3: Gezund un Lebn, *New York, 1905*

The journal *Gezund un Lebn* (fig. 3) published in New York in 1905–06 by Dr. Leonard Landes, while not strictly vegetarian, encouraged vegetarianism and gave advice as well on how to be attractive to women ("be nice" and "offer compliments") ("Der Umgang Mit Froyen" 15), and warned against the dangers of drinking tea, criticizing people, talking too much, and cruelty to animals ("Tey Trinken" 63; "Tsufil Kritikirn Yenem" 19; "Redn Tsufil" 21; "Umgang Mit Khayes" 27). The cover of the first issue placed a photograph of a beautiful young woman in traditional dress looking after her cows in the center of a lavish Art Nouveau border, indicating that the editor looks to the future while continuing to cherish tradition.

Figure 4: Der Naturis (un Vegetarier), *New York, 1920*

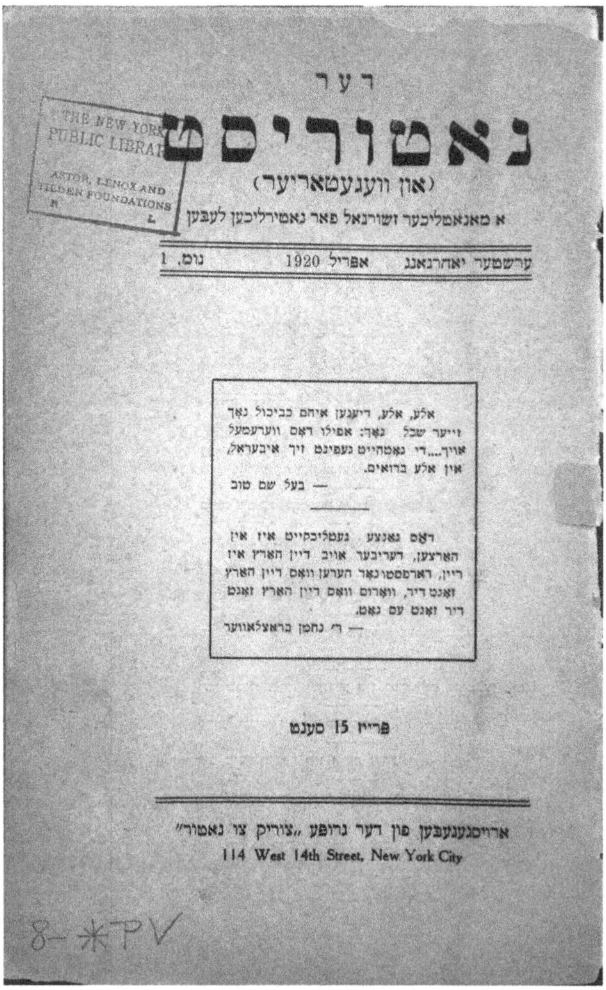

דער
נאטוריסט
(און וועגעטאריער)
א מאנאטליכער זשורנאל פאר נאטירליכען לעבען

ערשטער יאהרגאנג | אפריל 1920 | נום. 1

אלע, אלע, ריענען איהם כביכול נאך
זייער שכל נאך: אפילו דאס ווערעמעל
אויך...די גאטהייט געפינט זיך איבעראל,
אין אלע ברואים.
— בעל שם טוב

דאס גאנצע געטליכקייט איז אין
הארצען, דעריבער אויב דיין הארץ איז
ריין, דארפסטו נאר הערען וואס דיין הארץ
זאגט דיר, ווארום וואס דיין הארץ זאגט
דיר זאגט עס גאט.
— ר' נחמן בראצלאווער

פרייז 15 סענט

ארויסגעגעבען פון דער גרופע „צוריק צו נאטור"
114 West 14th Street, New York City

Der Naturist (*un Vegetarier*) (*The Naturist* [*and Vegetarian*]) (fig. 4) may be the earliest vegetarian journal published in Yiddish. It offered only one recipe in its first and only issue. The recipe was for a "tsimes" made with grated raw apple, brown sugar, and cinnamon, and came with a promise that more substantial dishes from Jewish and American cuisine would be forthcoming in future issues (Littauer 28). The questions and answers column advised that the only vegetarian part of Swiss cheese is the holes (29).[8] The front cover had quotations from the Baal Shem Tov and Rabbi Nakhman of Bratslav, revered figures of the Hasidic world, hinting that the editor might have taken inspiration from religious sources, but the content of the journal is entirely secular, quoting extensively from Lev Tolstoy, Rabindranath Tagore, and the American Transcendentalists.

Figure 5: Di Vegetarishe Velt: A Monatshrift far der Humanitarishn Gedank, *New York, 1921*

The hyper-modern design of *Di Vegetarishe Velt* (fig. 5) shows that this journal is all about the future. A recipe column by "Mulb-A-Dlog," probably a pseudonym for the editor-in-chief, Haym Goldblum, offers recipes for "Ge-vedzh" (*ghivetch*, a Balkan vegetable stew), a potato and barley sauce, and an ingenious recipe for a pea soup and roast, in which the pea-broth is the base for a vegetable soup, and the cooked peas, mixed with eggs and corn flakes (!), are made into a roast to be stuffed with a savory mushroom and onion stuffing (27–28). The second issue has recipes for spinach, asparagus, salsify, cauliflower, and artichokes (25–27). The editors looked toward the future in their editorials about identity and feeling, and address as well the problems of the present, such as the draconian immigration laws enacted in 1920 (Horowitz 1). The journal published reviews, stories, and poems, and, in the first issue, "The Vegetarian Hymn" (fig. 6).

Figure 6: Vegetarisher Himn *from Issue 1 of* Di Vegetarishe Velt

The Vegetarian Hymn

Chorus:

Blessed be he
Blessed be he
Who regards life with mercy
Blessed be he
Blessed be he
Who feels the pain and suffering of others

Solo:

Blessed be he
Who has the power
To eat no flesh and spill no blood
Blessed be he
Whose humane heart
Protects every creature
From woe and pain
Blessed be he
Who considers, who strives
Who seeks spirit in all
And just like a mentsh, lives. (Horowitz 1)

The author of this hymn appropriates the formal structures of Jewish prayer to deliver a primarily secular message rooted in the Yiddish cultural and ethical humanism. The reiteration of "Blessed be He" relocates the center of gratitude and agency from the divine to the human being making an ethical choice.

The hymn is arranged for a mixed chorus and tenor soloist. Choral singing had become an enormously popular activity among American Jews who associated with progressive movements and such workers' choruses as The Workmen's Circle Chorus (associated with a socialist institution) and the Jewish People's Philharmonic Chorus (associated with the Communist Party) (Schappes 234–35).

Figure 7: Vegetarizm *by Elisee Reclus, 1921*

Chayyim Goldblum's introduction to his translation of Elisee Reclus's *Vegetarizm* (fig. 7) notes that mistreatment of animals is inseparable from mistreatment of one's fellow humans. Reclus starts from personal experience to address the issues facing the newly reformed world (13).

Figure 8: Der Vegetarisher Gedank, *Los Angeles, 1930*

Two very different writers made the case for vegetarianism as the food of the future in the pages of the journal *Der Vegetarisher Gedank* (*Vegetarian Thought*) (fig. 8). In the first issue, Melech Ravitch wrote:

> We vegetarians are people of the future. We are not heroes or martyrs. Anyone who willingly decides to be a vegetarian even for just a week finds in vegetarianism great joy, inner happiness and often, the greatest delight in one's life. What kind of heroism is it not to want to be a graveyard for animals? What kind of martyrdom is it to be happy?
>
> But we are people of the future because of our sharp, piercing insight to see the suffering of others, because the person of the present can see everything except suffering. (5)

Sholem Aleichem, in his very own style, made a similar point in a letter to Joseph Perper:

> What a remarkable coincidence! Just as I received your lovely letter, I received a letter from Dr. Zamenhof, the mastermind of Esperanto, asking my permission to publish some of my stories in Esperanto. Vegetarianism and Esperanto stem from the same ideological root. I am utterly convinced that very soon, nu, let's say in a thousand or two thousand years, all people will be vegetarian, all will speak one language, Esperanto, and all will observe one faith, Judaism, of course.
>
> What interests me as a Jew is if all the people in the world were suddenly to adopt your faith, (that is, vegetarianism), including the Jews, (I hope that by THEN our rights will be the same as all mortals, even in the "Jewish Pale")[9] what would be the lamentable fate of our kosher butchers, and rabbis, and the question about kosher and unkosher, and all the discussion on meat and milk, and the *milkhik* plate and the *fleyshik* pot, and the meat tax?[10] My God, what an upheaval! I am not joking. (Perper 2)

Of course, he *is* joking but, in the larger sense, it is no joke. Sholem Aleichem is making gentle sport of the wide-eyed idealism and heartbreaking hopefulness of the Esperantists and vegetarians. Perper seems to have taken the letter quite literally.

No recipes or any discussion of food or cooking appear in the four issues of *Der Vegetarisher Gedank*, and all the contributions are by men, though one article "Di froy als vegetarier" ("The Woman As a Vegetarian") addresses the forces attracting and repelling women from vegetarianism:

> The woman lags behind the man philosophically and is reluctant to embrace new ideological intellectual movements . . . women are more conservative than men . . . too often the woman is the slave to the family's needs . . . It is hard to fight the meat eater in the woman, almost impossible to steer her off the *fleyshik*, bloody path.
>
> But she has positive characteristics. It is not her nature to be a drunkard or glutton. She is gentle and full of sympathy. She is no slave to food like the man who has to have his schnapps before dinner, his beefsteak for dinner, and his cigar after dinner. (Pinsker)

The futurists of the Jewish vegetarian movement seem to have been stuck solidly in the past as far as women were concerned. The remark about a woman being "slave to the family's needs" seems to be a perfect opportunity to address the practical issues of shopping, cooking, and eating for vegetarians, but the author does not see these to be issues that would be relevant to women considering vegetarianism. No recipes or any articles related to food, cooking, eating, or provisioning appeared in any issue of *Der Vegetarisher Gedank*. It is possible that the recipe writer "Mulb-A-Dlog" of *Di Vegetarishe Velt* felt the need to use a pseudonym because he or she felt that recipes were not as serious or worthy as his or her other writing.

Figure 9: Dos Kol fun dem Vegetarier, *New York, 1952*

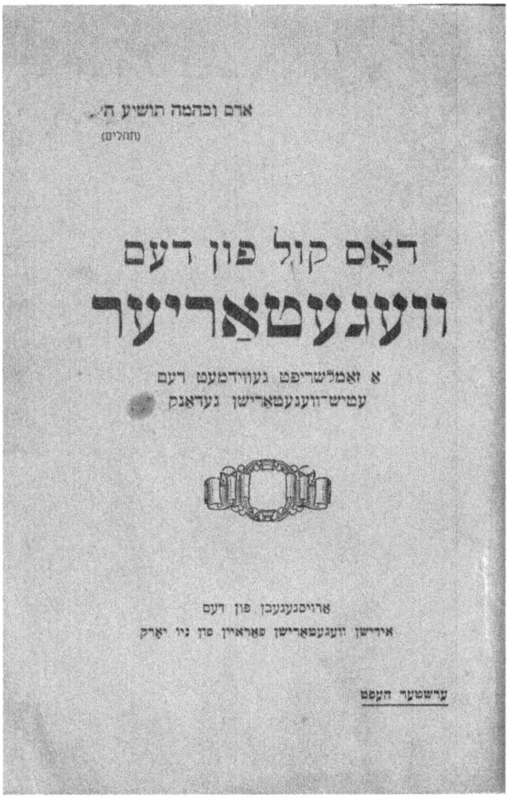

The editors of *Dos kol fun dem vegetarier* (*The Voice of the Vegetarian*) (fig. 9) (Davis) follow the path that Aaron Frankel had set out in choosing vegetarianism for ethical reasons, but rather than drawing examples from Jewish sacred texts, they look to the classics and modern secular literature to provide a humanist ethical vegetarian point of view. This booklet includes essays by Melech Ravitch and Tolstoy, a poem by Kadia Molodowsky, and fragments from Plutarch and Ovid translated into Yiddish.[11] "The Vegetarian Hymn," by J. Pirazhnikoff, is the concluding chapter (fig. 10).

Figure 10: Vegetarian Hymn from Dos Kol fun dem Vegetarier

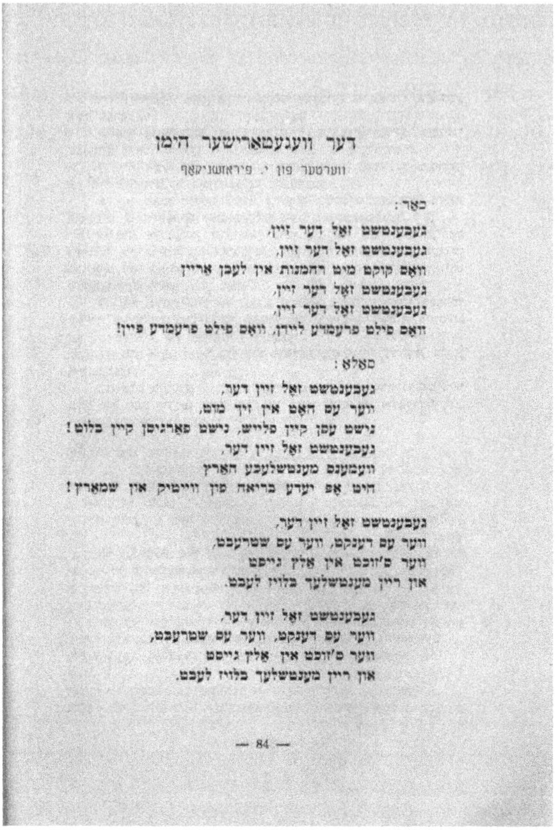
דער וועגעטאַרישער הימן

ווערטער פון י. פּיראָזשניקאָף

כאָר:

געבענטשט זאָל דער זיין,
געבענטשט זאָל דער זיין,
וואָס קוקט מיט רחמנות אין לעבן אַריין
געבענטשט זאָל דער זיין,
געבענטשט זאָל דער זיין,
וואָס פילט פרעמדע ליידן, וואָס פילט פרעמדע פיין!

סאָלאָ:

געבענטשט זאָל זיין דער,
ווער עס האָט אין זיך מוט,
נישט עסן קיין פלייש, נישט פאַרגיסן קיין בלוט!
געבענטשט זאָל זיין דער,
וועמענס מענטשלעכע האַרץ
היט אָפּ יעדע בריאה פון ווייטיק און שמאַרץ!

געבענטשט זאָל זיין דער,
ווער עס דענקט, ווער עס שטרעבט,
ווער ס'זוכט אין אַלץ גייסט
און ריין מענטשלעך בלויז לעבט.

געבענטשט זאָל זיין דער,
ווער עס דענקט, ווער עס שטרעבט,
ווער ס'זוכט אין אַלץ גייסט
און ריין מענטשלעך בלויז לעבט.

— 84 —

Figure 11: Grave of Menahem Morgenstern, New Mount Carmel Cemetery, New York

The same brilliant juxtaposition of traditional Jewish religious form and secular vegetarian content appears on Menahem Morgenstren's tombstone in New Mount Carmel Cemetery in Queens (fig. 11).[12] The epitaph reads:

> Benjamin Menahem Nakhke Morgenstern
> Ethical Vegetarian
> (May his soul be bound up in the bonds of life)
> The Torah of truth was in his mouth and no injustice was ever found on his lips;
> he walked in peace and righteousness, and no injustice was ever on his lips; he walked in truth and righteousness, and he turned many away from sin.

The verses are a Yiddish translation from the opening of the book of Micah. Taking a path that goes opposite to the usual Jewish method of reading texts, looking for abstract metaphors in concrete examples, this epitaph selects an abstract quotation and makes it very concrete. The Torah of truth was in Morgenstern's actual, ethically-inclined mouth. No injustice was on his actual lips because he did not eat meat. Whether Morgenstern was a husband and father (his obituary in *Dos kol fun dem vegeterairer* indicates he was) (Davis 6) is not mentioned on his monument, which memorializes only his devotion to ethical vegetarianism.

Figure 12: Do we have to eat meat? *New York, 1956*

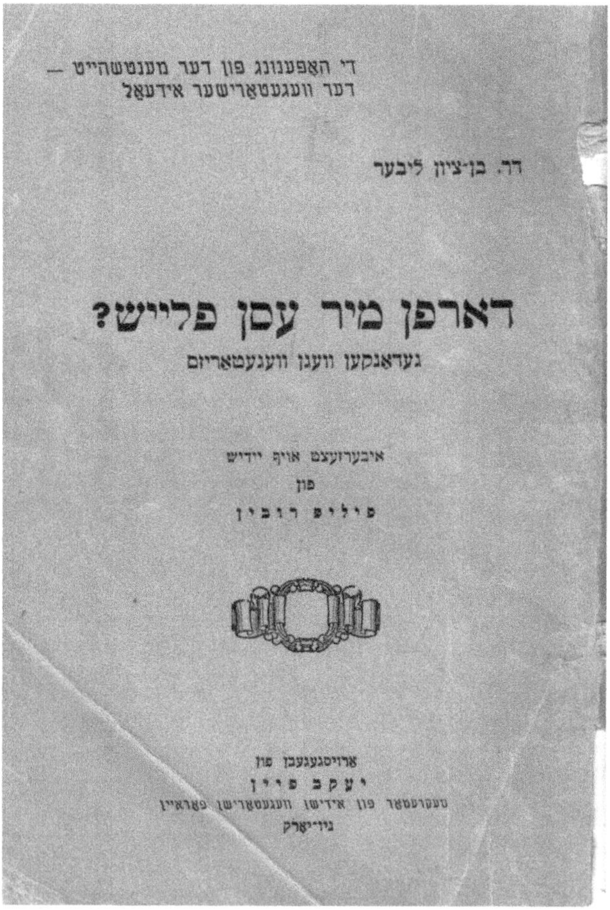

די האָפענונג פון דער מענטשהייט —
דער וועגעטאַרישער אידעאַל

דר. בן-ציון ליבער

דארפן מיר עסן פלייש?

געדאנקען וועגן וועגעטאריזם

איבערזעצט אויף יידיש
פון
פיליפ רובין

אַרויסגעגעבן פון
יעקב פיין
טעקרעטאַר פון אידישן וועגעטאַרישן פאַראיין
ניו-יאָרק

The vegetarian polemic *Darfn mir esn fleysh*? (Do we have to eat meat?) by Benzion Liber (fig. 12) is also primarily concerned with ethical issues related to meat consumption. *Darfn mir esn fleysh*? sees the killing of animals as a danger not only to the souls of the humans involved but also to the very civilization which allows such a practice to continue. This move to extend the moral concern of vegetarianism to include the societal consequences of individual food choices intimates the increasing relevance of the role of social activism related to rejecting meat. Vegetarian cookbooks present opposition to conventional food practices (Miller and Hardman 111–12) and, in so doing, present opposition to cold convention itself.

Figure 13: Originele Yidishe Familyen Kokh Bukh, *undated, circa 1920*

דער
אריגינאלער אידישער פאמיליען
קאך בוך

אריגינעל פערפאסט פון א אידישע פרוי, וועלכע האט 45 יאהר
ערפאהרונג אין איראפעאישער און אמעריקאנישער קיך.
די קונסט צו באקען און קאכען ריין אידישע מאכלים און
בעסטע געריכטען קאן יעדע אידישע פרוי אויסלערנען דורך
דיעזען קאך בוך, וועלכער איז ניט איבערזעצט פון קיין אנדער
שפראך, נאר אריגינעל פערפאסט אין אידיש פון

הינדע אמחאניטצקי

דריטע פארבעסערטע און פארמעהרטע אויפלאגע.

אין צווייטען טהייל פון בוך זיינען צוגעגעבען פאלגענדע קאפיטלאך:

1. ווידזשעטייבעל און וועגעטארישע מאכלים.
2. א ריינע האוזונג.
3. ווי צו האלטען די הויז ווירטשאפט אין ארדנונג.
4. וואס צו עסען און וואס צו טרינקען אין די הייסע זומער מאנאטען.
5. ווי צו האלטען א סטריקטלי כשר קיטשען.

ארויסגעגעבען פון ש. דרוקערמאנ'ס בוכהאנדלונג
50 קאנעל סטריט, ניו יארק.

Published by
S. DRUCKERMAN, 50 Canal St., New York

Hinde Amchanitzki was a chef and restaurateur who had some fame as a cookbook author in her lifetime and had another moment of renewed fame in

2010 when her tombstone, which for unknown reasons had never been placed on her grave, was discovered on the Lower East Side (Roberts).

Amchanitzki's *Ler-bukh vi azoy tsu kokhn un bakn* was published in 1901. A second edition, titled *Origineler Yidisher familyen kokh bukh*, most probably edited by her daughter, came out about twenty years later (the second book is undated) (fig. 13). The second edition differs from the first in that it has added sections on "Vedzsheteybel un vegetarish makholim" (vegetable and vegetarian foods) reflecting the currency vegetarianism had gained in the first decades of the twentieth century. Traditional northeastern Yiddish recipes from Amchanitzki's native region such as sweet jams made from beets and radishes are joined by recipes for health foods such as "Graham bread," "Hygienic yeast bread," nut cutlets, bean cutlets, and pineapple sorbet. None of Amchanitzki's meat recipes are deleted from the later edition, and nothing in her book suggests that she shares Frankel's opinions on slaughter. The inclusion of vegetarian and health-food recipes seems to be an attempt by her daughter to bring the book up-to-date and was probably entirely market-driven.[13]

Figure 14: Vegetarishe Kokh Bukh "Ratsionale Narung," *New York, 1926*

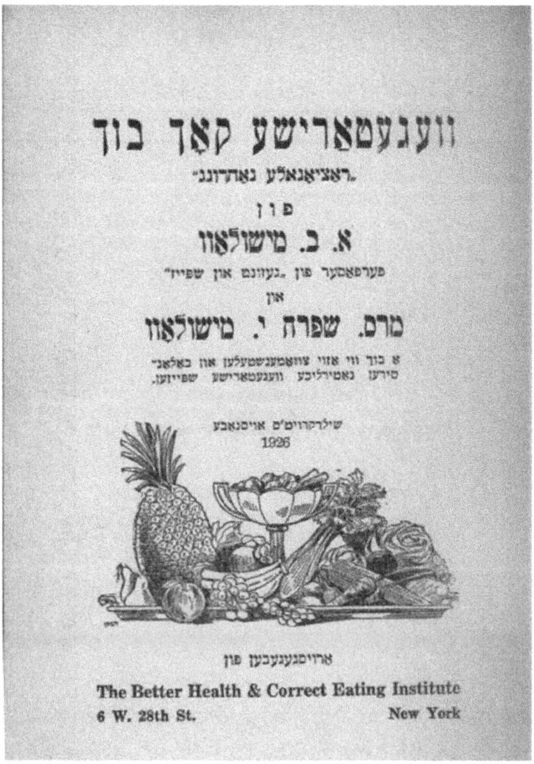

Abraham Mishulow's *Gezunt un Shpayz* (*Health and Nutrition*) and its companion volume, Abraham and Shifra Mishelow's *Vegetarishe Kokhbukh "Ratsionale Nahrung"* (*Vegetarian Cook Book "Rational Nourishment"*) (fig. 14) were both published in 1926. The gorgeous graphic on the title page, with its lush plenitude of fresh fruits and vegetables, is typical of images found on menus in Yiddish dairy and vegetarian restaurants and resorts of the first half of the twentieth century. Dairy restaurants (which served fish, but no meat) and vegetarian restaurants (where no fish was served) and resorts like the Vita-Ray House in Freeland New Jersey, owned by Victor and Hannah Tofilowsky, Hamburger's Evergreen Vegetarian Health Farm in Farmingdale, NJ, The Vegetarian Health Food Resort in Bushkill, PA, and Shaffer's Vegetarian Hotel in Woodridge New York, were very popular, attracting clients, many or even most of whom were not vegetarian. The first volume begins with a poem "Why I am a vegetarian!" (punctuation in the original) by Herman Schildkraut, and continues with an essay by Mishulow on food, exercise and disease. The second volume includes many recipes by Shifra Mishulow. Mishelow's recipes make use of some ingredients that may still have been exotic to American cooks, such as asparagus, Brussels sprouts, salsify, tomatoes, and even kale (a vegetable that in 1926 had not yet had its Cinderella moment). Recipes such as those for sandwiches, chowders, and a "Hamburger Omelet" (a two-layer omelet of yolks mixed with breadcrumbs topped with whipped egg whites) are mostly drawn from American cookery and health food cookery, but a few Jewish dishes, such as kugels (called *teygekhts* here) and some interesting hybrids, such as pumpkin *Flodn*, are included.[14] Both books feature ads for health foods and meat substitutes such as Protose and Nutose.

Readers familiar with the names Protose and Nutose from Moshe Nadir's satirical story noted below may be surprised, as I was, to learn that Protose and Nutose were actual meat substitutes available in the twentieth century. Along with Nutolin and Savita, they were created by John Harvey Kellogg, most famous for having invented flaked breakfast cereal, made by the Battle Creek Food Company, later Kellogg's (Shprintzen).

The Mishelows argue that a vegetarian diet is the best and most rational diet. In his introduction Abraham Mishelow invokes Hippocrates and discusses the importance of introducing scientific nutrition to the Yiddish reader. In her introduction, Shifra Mishelow invokes Dr. Pavlov, speaks of the importance of the appearance and flavor of food as well as its nutritional value, and makes the interesting point that a meat-based diet is actually more limited than a diet based on vegetables. Her colorful palette of vegetable dishes makes the case for the variety possible in a vegetarian kitchen. While the Mishelows' inclusion of Schildkraut's poem shows them to be sympathetic to the humanitarian case for vegetarianism, it is their dedication to science and reason that drives their choices.

The Mishelows' argument that a vegetarian diet is both healthy and rational allowed the vegetarians of the early twentieth century to reclaim some of the power over their bodies and lives that they may have feared surrendered to the bewildering technological advances in science and industry. By choosing vegetarianism, they could put into action their ethical and ideological concerns to meet the advances of the future while simultaneously providing a mechanism to address the very anxieties these advances provoked.

Figure 15: Protose and Nutose from Gezunt un Shpayz, *1926*

Figure 16: Kokh-Bukh far Gezuntheyt, *New York, 1931*

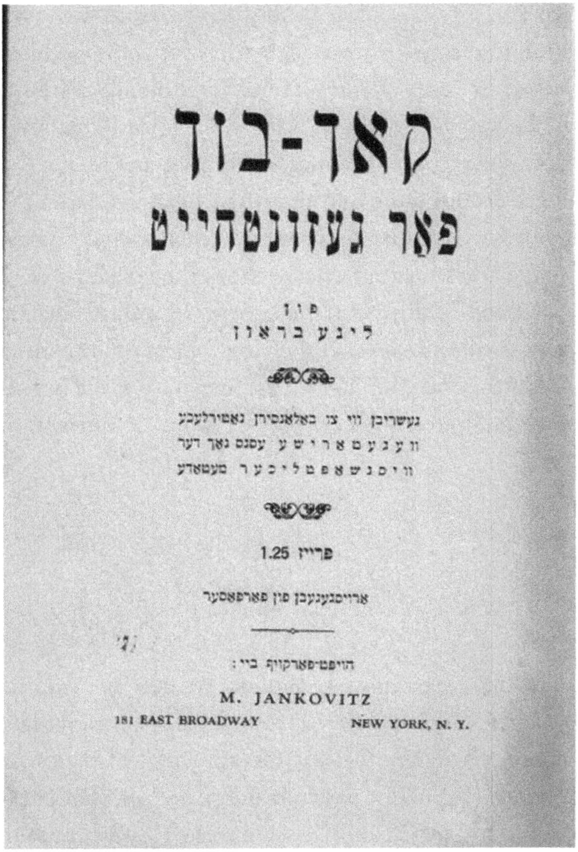

קאך-בוך
פאר געזונטהייט

פון
לינע בראון

געשריבן ווי צו באלאנסירן נאטירלעכע
וועגעטארישע עסנס נאך דער
וויסנשאפטליכער מעטאדע

פרייז 1.25

ארויסגעגעבן פון פארפאסער

הויפט-פארקויף ביי:

M. JANKOVITZ
181 EAST BROADWAY NEW YORK, N. Y.

Lena Brown's 1931 *Kokh Bukh far gezuntheyt* (*Cook Book for Health*) begins with a poem "people awake" warning of the dangers not only of "bad foods" but also "bad drinks, drug, and dope." While the Mishelows promote vegetarianism because it is rational, Brown's approach to vegetarianism is solidly based on health. "Our civilized cuisine," she writes, "does us great harm" (9). Brown's cuisine, featuring latkes, knishes, blintzes, and *teygelekh* is closer to traditional Eastern European Jewish cooking than Shifra Mishelow's but there is also avocado salad, dandelion salad, and a "Greek salad" made with cabbage, carrots, peppers, apples, tomatoes and olives. The book includes a recipe for vegetarian gefilte fish, showing that Brown was sensitive to the challenges faced by Jewish homemakers, and which dishes they could not live without. The main ingredient for Brown's vegetarian gefilte fish is what she calls "oyster plent" (oyster plant or salsify).[15] Brown's recipe for stuffed vegetable turkey provides a list of ingredients and then directs the cook to "make it look like a turkey" (Brown 69).

In addition to recipes, Brown offers fifty-five commandments for health (e.g., "eat enough raw fruits and vegetables," "get plenty of fresh air"), tips for caring for one's hair, nails, teeth, and skin, and a guide to bathing (39–43).[16] In her introduction, she recounts coming to America and seeing that people had become estranged from nature and that their health suffered as a result. Her argument for vegetarianism is as a cure for the exhausted bodies of industrial workers. Brown's back-to-nature ethos echoes the concerns of contemporary writers like Kallet and Schlink that the benefits of industrialization and modernization are not without costs. Her championing of all-natural ingredients (no Protose or Nutose appear in her book) may have made her seem old-fashioned at the time, but in retrospect make her the most futuristic of all the writers cited herein.

THE LEGACY

I know of only one vegetarian cookbook written in Yiddish after 1950, Eisenberger's *Maykholim Tsum Gezunt* (Food for Health), privately published in 1989. Eisenberger is an heir to Lena Brown, Shifra Mishelow, and "Mulb-a-Dlog" in her energy, originality, passion, and generosity, but not by any means in her ideology. Eisenberger belongs to New York's Hasidic community, and was inspired to try vegetarian cooking only for health reasons after reading Adele Davis. Since Jewish law permits eating meat, it would be unseemly to consider another practice more compassionate (Jochnowitz, "Health, Revolution and a *Yidisher Tam*" 54).

If Eisenberger is not an heir to the Yiddish vegetarian writers of the early twentieth century, neither are contemporary Jewish vegetarian writers who see vegetarianism as the logical completion of *halacha*, Jewish religious practice (Schwartz; see also *Jewish Veg*; Kalechofsky and Rasiel). The writers who are the closest heirs to Mishelow and Brown among second and third wave vegetarians are the authors of *The Political Palate Cookbooks* by the Bloodroot Collective (Bloodroot Collective et al., *Political Palate*; Beaven et al., *Second Seasonal Political Palate*; Beaven et al., *Perennial Political Palate*), who explicitly link radical eating to radical thinking, and show great fondness for traditional Jewish cooking.

THE BACKLASH

The mainstream Jewish press, especially the Yiddish dailies *The Forward, Varheit,* and *Der Tog,* was more likely to look upon growing enthusiasm for vegetarianism as a threat to continuity in Jewish cooking. Dr. Melech Chmelnitzki warned readers about "the flaws and dangers of a vegetarian diet" (6). An article in the English-language supplement to *The Forward* in 1929 expressed concern that American fads like "the Almighty Salad" and mayonnaise were winning Jews away from traditional dishes. It concluded:

> And if Mother, in her zeal to take off pounds, turns Vegetarian, in come the protoses and the nutoses to add to Father's woes. As if it were not enough that the good old hunk of *gefilte* fish has been emasculated! As if he didn't suffer enough pain from missing the good old aroma of goosefat, now that mother uses Crisco! But if he asks for some herring, he'll get anchovies. And anything, oh, anything, for some *kasha varnishkes*! But no—the calories forbid it. (Berg)

The article does not even consider that vegetarianism is rooted in anything but the desire to "take off pounds." Both vegetarianism and dietary innovations in general are introduced by "mother," and it is Father who is missing the good old ways. The dismissal of vegetarian concerns as simply "female" and the description of men as victims of the whims of the female household cook points out an interesting power dynamic. While it may be that men run the editorial pages, women are making executive decisions and fostering integration into American society.

Figure 17: "Vi Azoy a Fraydenker Shlogt Kapores," Der Sheygets, *1930*

Cookbooks, pamphlets, and menus in Yiddish show only that a number of Yiddish speakers were interested in vegetarianism. Vegetarian restaurants and resorts may have catered to a largely non-vegetarian clientele. The most convincing evidence of the presence and relevance of the Yiddish vegetarian movement is to be found not in the work of its proponents but in the opposition. The popular press in the early decades of the twentieth century found vegetarians and vegetarianism to provide fertile ground for sport. In the cartoon above, "How a freethinker performs the *Kaparoth* ceremony," a "freethinker," dressed in modern clothing but identifiably Jewish, holds his hands over the head of a rooster in the position of a parent blessing a child on the eve of the Sabbath and says: "May you have a good year, dear chicken, may you know of no trouble, and may I be your atonement!" (fig. 17).[17]

In "Nutose un Protose" Moshe Nadir skewered vegetarians and vegetarian restaurant dishes made from Protose and Nutose in particular. In the story, the imprisoned narrator relates the events leading up to his crime. At the urging of a friend who tells him "your body is a graveyard!" he tried a vegetarian restaurant where all the dishes were made with Protose and Nutose. After choosing between Protose soup or Nutose soup, Protose steak or Nutose steak, Protose or Nutose side dishes and Protose or Nutose beverages, he goes mad and it is finally revealed that he is in jail for killing the waiter.

"The Grossmans," Isaac Rosenfeld's comic and elegiac memoir of a family falling into dysfunction, finds in their kitchen the seeds of their despair:

> I too go to the kitchen, on the way passing the bedroom where, when I look in, I see a heap of soiled underwear on the bed. Ada's presence is palpable in the kitchen. These are her knives hanging blade down from a rack, her dishes, her pots and pans, her pantry, loaded with health foods, Nutose, Protose, dried figs, jars of wild honey, products of Battle Creek.

Figure 18: "In a Vegetarisher Restorant" from The Forward, *1917*

This strip, titled "In a vegetarian restaurant" ("In a Vegetarisher Restorant") (fig. 18) has five panels, reading right to left.[18] A customer is seated at a table in a restaurant with a portrait of Leo Tolstoy on the wall. In the first panel, the waiter says, "Believe me, mister, I will give you a piece of vegetarian fish that you will enjoy so much, you'll think it's real." The customer is unimpressed, but in the second panel he admits that it does indeed look like real fish, and the waiter adds that it is impossible to distinguish from real fish. In the third the customer enthusiastically says the vegetarian fish is even better than real fish and asks if the waiter can bring a cement steak. In the fourth panel, he is enjoying the steak; even the bones seem real. In the fifth panel, the scene shifts to the kitchen where the chef is slaughtering a turkey, and the caption helpfully explains that the reason the food tastes so good is that it is real meat. The elaborate con is therefore vegetarianism itself.

These bitter satirical takes on vegetarians and vegetarian food are evidence that even while Yiddish-speaking vegetarians may have been few in number, their cultural significance was disproportionately large. While most American Jewish immigrants and their children may not have chosen vegetarianism, they were stirred by the same impulses to improve themselves and their society. Striving to be more moral or more rational, healthier or happier, closer to Jewish tradition or closer to classical civilization, Jewish Americans in the early twentieth century believed they could make a saner, safer future, and could do so by saner and safer eating.

Notes

* I am grateful to Amanda Miriam Khaye Seigel of the New York Public Library for her extraordinary efforts.

1. *Di Tsukunft* in Mlotek et al. (86–87).
2. Two works that expressed these concerns are Kallet and Schlink, and Schlink, cited in Levenstein.
3. Jews were by no means the only population seeking an optimistic food future. In 1932, the artist and activist Filippo Marinetti wrote in his *Futurist Cookbook*: "The Futurist culinary revolution has the lofty, noble and universally expedient aim of changing radically the eating habits of our race, strengthening it, dynamizing it and spiritualizing it with brand new food combinations. . . . Until now men have fed themselves like ants, rats, cats or oxen. . . . It is not by chance that this work is published during a world economic crisis, which has clearly inspired a dangerous and depressing panic. . . . We propose as an antidote to this panic a Futurist way of cooking, that is: optimism at the table!" (21).
4. Alter-Sholem Kacyzne, 1885–1941, was a photographer famous for the masterwork *Poyln*, a book of photographs of Jewish life in prewar Poland. He was also a writer and poet.
5. I am grateful to William Oshrin for bringing this book to my attention.
6. Bloshteyn; see Kirshenblatt-Gimblett, "Cookbooks." The earliest printed books in Yiddish were religious manuals for women published in Krakow in 1534–35. See Turniansky.
7. The title page indicates that the book is a translation from an 1896 English version, but while copies of the Yiddish translation can be found in several major collections, I have as yet been unable to turn up a copy of the English original. The English original must have been a very different book. *Loy Tirtsah* relies heavily on such Yiddish narrative techniques as *Ivri-Taytsh*, beginning a sentence with a line in Hebrew from scripture and then translating or explaining it in Yiddish, that it would be difficult and awkward in English. The book is heavily salted and peppered as well with untranslated biblical verses that the reader is expected to recognize without explanation.
8. It is unclear whether Littauer was concerned with non-vegetarian rennet used to make cheese or if he was in fact an early vegan. The journal has many baffling jokes the editor clearly found hilarious.
9. The Pale of Settlement—the part of Eastern Europe occupied by the Russian Empire in the eighteenth, nineteenth and early twentieth centuries, including most of Poland and Ukraine, and all of Lithuania, Latvia, Belarus, and Moldova.
10. The taxes on kosher meat levied by Jewish communities were a source of bitter dissension and targets of reformers in the old country. Mendele Moykher Sforim's 1869 play *Di Takse* is a biting satirical take on the subject.

11. Meylekh Ravitsh (1893–1976) is famous for modernist poetry and essays as well as his memoirs, in which he recounts his adoption of vegetarianism. Lev Tolstoy (1828–1910), the world-renowned Russian novelist and reformer, was especially revered in Jewish vegetarian circles (see fig. 18). Kadia Molodowski (1894–1975) wrote poetry and essays on literary and political matters. She was a fierce critic of Yiddish writers who failed to treat the work of their female colleagues seriously. Plutarch (46–120 BCE) was a historian who argued for vegetarianism on moral and physiological grounds. Ovid (43 BCE–17 CE) was a poet and disciple of Pythagoras.
12. I came upon Morgenstern's monument purely by chance. I was visiting the grave of the Yiddish poet Anna Margolin, close by.
13. The later edition of the book was published commercially and more widely advertised than the first, but the vegetarian recipes may not be entirely responsible for its success.
14. *Flodn*, or *fludn*, is a flaky, multi-layered pastry filled with lemon preserves, apples, walnuts, or poppy seeds. See Jochnowitz, "All You Need Is a Potato."
15. Salsify is also mentioned in Mulb-A-Dlog, "Di Vegetarishe Kikh," no. 2 (26), Mishulow and Mishulow (84–85), and in Liber (26). Liber calls the vegetable *salsifay*. The Yiddish word for this vegetable is *tsign-berdl*, or goat's beard, but the Mishelows, Brown and Liber all seem to have encountered it first in English. I have prepared Brown's recipe for vegetarian gefilte fish. It is delicious and can fool ardent fish enthusiasts.
16. The section on bathing includes showers, hot baths, cold baths, and also "air baths." Brown urges her readers to spend at least a few minutes a day walking around naked.
17. *Shlogn kapores* is the practice of waving a living chicken over one's head in the days immediately before Yom Kippur (the day of atonement) while reciting the formula "This is my substitute, my atonement. This chicken will die while I will begin a good long life and peace." The prayer is part of the high holiday liturgy, but at least since the thirteenth century such distinguished rabbis as the Rashba have held the practice to be pagan superstition and Joseph Karo, the sixteenth-century author of the code of Jewish law *Shulhan Arukh* urged the abandonment of this "foolish custom." See, for instance, Bloch (160).
18. This strip probably appeared in *The Forward* in 1917. The undated clipping is from the Zuni Maud collection at YIVO. I am grateful to Eddy Portnoy for bringing this document to my attention.

Works Cited

Amchanitzki, H. *Der Origineler Idisher Familyen Kokh Bukh*. nd.

———. *Lehr-Bukh Vi Azoy Tsu Kokhen Un Baken*. 1901.

Beaven, Betsey et al. *The Second Seasonal Political Palate: A Feminist Vegetarian Cookbook*. Sanguinaria, 1984.

———. *The Perennial Political Palate: The Third Feminist Vegetarian Cookbook*. Sanguinaria, 1993.

Berg, Temmy. "Jewish Cooking on the Wane." *Forward*, 14 April 1929, p. 6.

Bloch, Abraham P. *The Biblical and Historical Background of the Jewish Holy Days*. KTAV, 1977.

Bloodroot Collective et al. *The Political Palate: A Feminist Vegetarian Cookbook* Sanguinaria, 1980.

Bloshteyn, O. *Kokh-Bukh Far Yudishe Froyen*. Matz, 1896.

Brown, Lena. *Kokh-Bukh Far Gezuntheyt*. Jankovitz, 1931.

Chmelnitzki, Melech. "Iz Fleysh an Umnatirlekh Ernarung Far Menshen." *Jewish Daily Forward*, 30 June 1929, p. 6.

Davis, Nathan Samuel. *Dos Kol Fun Dem Vegetarier*. New York, 1952.

Eisenberger, Malky. *Food for Health Cookbook*. Eindruk, 1991.

———. *Maykholim Tsum Gezunt: Mit Ariber 100 Retseptn*. Eindruk, 1989.

Frankel, Aaron H. *Lo Tirtsah: Eyn Obhandlung Iber Vegetaryanizm*. Rabinovits, 1899. 4 vols.

Green, Joe. *The Jewish Vegetarian Tradition*. 2nd ed., Johannesburg, 1969. Microform.

Harshav, Benjamin. *The Meaning of Yiddish*. Univ. of California, 1990.

Horowitz, Isaac. "Komentarn." *Di Vegetarishe Velt*, vol. 1, no. 2, 1921, p. 1.

Jewish Veg, www.jewishveg.org. Accessed 21 Sept. 2017.

Jochnowitz, Eve. "All You Need Is a Potato: The Culinary Performances of Grushenka Abramova." *Women and Performance*, vol. 21, no. 3, 2011, pp. 367–84.

———. "Feasting on the Future: Foods of the World of Tomorrow at the New York World's Fair of 1939–40." *Performance Research*, vol. 4, no. 1, 1999, pp. 110–20.

———. "Health, Revolution and a *Yidisher Tam*: Reading Yiddish Vegetarian Cookbooks as Women's Literature." *Di Froyen: Women and Yiddish*, edited by Purlaine Lieberman, Jewish Women's Resource Center, 1997, pp. 52–56.

Kacyzne, Alter. "Vegtarizm Iz a Private Zakh." *Der Vegetarisher Gedank*, vol. 1, no. 3, March 1930, pp. 5–6.

Kalechofsky, Roberta, and Rosa Rasiel. *The Jewish Vegetarian Year Cookbook*. Micah, 1997.

Kallet, Arthur, and F. J. Schlink. *100,000,000 Guinea Pigs: Dangers in Everyday Foods, Drugs, and Cosmetics*. Vanguard, 1933.

Kirshenblatt-Gimblett, Barbara. "Cookbooks." *YIVO Encyclopedia of Jews in Eastern Europe*, 2010, www.yivoencyclopedia.org/article.aspx/Cookbooks. Accessed 30 Aug. 2017.

———. "Kitchen Judaism." *Getting Comfortable in New York: The American Jewish Home, 1880–1950*, edited by Susan L Braunstein and Jenna Weissman Joselit, Indiana Univ., 1990, pp. 75–105.

Landes, Leonard. "Der Umgang Mit Froyen." *Gezund un Lebn*, vol. 1, no. 1, Nov. 1905, p. 15.

———. "Redn Tsufil." *Gezund un Lebn*, vol. 1, no. 1, Nov. 1905, p. 21.

———. "Tey Trinken." *Gezund un Lebn*, vol. 1, no. 4, Feb. 1906, p. 63.

———. "Tsufil Kritikirn Yenem." *Gezund un Lebn*, vol. 1, no. 1, Nov. 1905, p. 19.

———. "Umgang Mit Khayes." *Gezund un Lebn*, vol. 1, no. 1, 1905, p. 27.

Levenstein, Harvey A. *Paradox of Plenty: A Social History of Eating in Modern America*. Oxford Univ., 1993.

Liber, Benzion. *Darfn Mir Esn Fleysh? Gedanken Vegn Vegetarianizm*. Translated by Philip Rubin, Jacob Fine, 1956.

Littauer, Moses Isaac. *Der Naturist (Un Vegetarier)*, vol. 1, no. 1, April 1920.

———. "Tsimes." *Der Naturist (Un Vegetarier)*, vol. 1, no. 1, 1920, p. 28.

Marinetti, F. T. *The Futurist Cookbook*. Bedford Arts, 1989.

Mendele Mokher Sforim. *Di Takse*. 1869. Play.

Miller, Laura J., and Emilie Hardman. "By the Pinch and Pound: Less and More Protest in American Vegetarian Cookbooks from the Nineteenth Century to the Present." *Protest on the Page: Essays on Print and the Culture of Dissent since 1865*, edited by James L. Baughman, Jennifer Ratner-Rosenhagen and James Philip Danky, Univ. of Wisconsin, 2015, pp. 111–36.

Mishulow, Abraham B. *Gezunt Un Shpayz*. New York, 1926.

Mishulow, Abraham B., and Shifrah I. Mishulow. *Vegetarishe Koch Buch*. New York, 1926.

Mlotek, Eleanor G. et al. *Songs of Generations: New Pearls of Yiddish Song*. New Workmen's Circle, 2004. [In Yiddish texts, with accompanying material in English and Yiddish.]

Mulb-A-Dlog. "Di Vegetarishe Kikh." *Di Vegetarishe Velt*, vol. 1, no. 2, 1921, pp. 25–27.

———. "Di Vegetarishe Kikh." *Di Vegetarishe Velt*, vol. 1, no. 1, 1921, pp. 22–28.

Nadir, Isaac Moishe. "Notus un Protus." *Oyf Gelekhter*. Verbe, 1919, pp. 74–79.

Nayes Folshtendiges Kokhbukh Fir Di Yidishe Kikhe: Ayn Unentberlikhes Handbukh Fir Yidish Froyen Und Tokhter Nebst Forshrift Fon Flaysh Kosher Makhen Und Khale Nemen, Iberhoypt Iber Raynlikhkayt Und Kashrut. Adalbert della Torre, 1854.

Perper, Joseph. "Sholem Aleichem Un Zayn Batsiung Tsum Vegetarizm." *Der Vegetarisher Gedank*, vol. 1, no. 3, March 1930, pp. 2–3.

Pinsker, V. "Di Froy Als Vegetarier." *Der Vegetarisher Gedank*, vol. 1, no. 2, 1930, pp. 5–6, 11.

Pirazshnikov, J. "Vegetarisher Himn." *Di Vegetarishe Velt*, vol. 1, no. 1, 1921, p. 13.

Poppendieck, Janet. *Breadlines Knee-Deep in Wheat: Food Assistance in the Great Depression*. Rutgers Univ., 1986.

Ravitch, Melech. "A Vort Vegn Nisht Fresn Fleysh." *Der Vegetarisher Gedank*, vol. 1, no. 1, Nov. 1929, pp. 5–6.

Reclus, Elisée, and Chayyim Goldblum. *Vegetarizm mit eynteylung un E. Reklu's biografye fun iberzetser.* Nyu Yorker Vegetarier Fareyn, 1921.

Rendsburg, Gary. "The Vegetarian Ideal in the Bible." *Food and Judaism*, edited by Leonard J. Greenspoon, Studies in Jewish Civilization, Creighton Univ., 2005, pp. 319–34.

Roberts, Sam. "The Curious Mystery of the Sidewalk Tombstone." *New York Times*, 8 July 2010, p. A19.

Rosenfeld, Isaac. "The Grossmans." *Southwest Review*, vol. 37, no. 3, Summer 1952, 212–20.

Schappes, Morris U. *The Jews in the United States: A Pictorial History, 1654 to the Present.* Citadel, 1958.

Schlink, F. J. *Eat, Drink and Be Wary*. Consumers' Research, 1935. Microform.

Schwartz, Richard H. *Judaism and Vegetarianism*. 1st ed., Exposition, 1982.

Shprintzen, Adam D. "Looks Like Meat, Smells Like Meat, Tastes Like Meat: Battle Creek, Protose and the Making of Modern Vegetarianism." *Food. Culture, and Society*, vol. 15, no. 1, 2012, pp. 113–28.

Turniansky, Chava. "Yiddish Literature before 1800." *YIVO Encyclopedia of Jews in Eastern Europe,* 2016, www.yivoencyclopedia.org/article.aspx/Yiddish_Literature/Yiddish_Literature_before_1800. Accessed 30 Aug. 2017.

"Vi Azoy a Fraydenker Shlogt Kapores." *Der Sheygets*, 3 Oct. 1930.

Ziegelman, Jane, and Andrew Coe. *A Square Meal: A Culinary History of the Great Depression*. 1st ed., HarperCollins, 2017.

Eating Up: The Origins of Bagels and Lox

by Jeffrey A. Marx

INTRODUCTION

To write about a food's history is always to write of its development; food and foodways are never static. Food evolves, travels, borrows, drops out of sight and then circles around after many years to be put on the table, again. To talk critically about a food, then, means that its earlier manifestations as well as its current ones must be taken into consideration. To write about a food's history is also to investigate its changing meaning to the communities that consume (or shun) it. Food's significance is never static, since, as Mintz has proposed, the power resting within ever-changing "outside meaning" (economic, social, and political conditions) sets the terms for the creation of "inside" symbolic meaning. Caution must therefore be exercised when food traditions and historical memories are involved, for they are not necessarily proof for actual events, especially when wrapped in the gauze of nostalgia (Fishman 6; Lederhendler 1–3; Mintz 20, 30; Trillin 53–54, 87–89; Wilk, *Home Cooking* 71–72; Wilk, "Paradoxes of Jews" 232).[1] This is especially true when looking at the history of bagels and lox.

The historical trajectory of bagels and lox (understood, for purposes of abbreviation, to include cream cheese as an ingredient, in the same way that "spaghetti and meatballs" is understood to include marinara sauce) has taken place over a four-hundred-year time span. As I will explore in this article, the combination's ingredients were an amalgamation of Jewish *and* Yankee foods that originated, respectively, in the early 1500s (the bagel) and the late 1800s (cream cheese and lox). Over an eighty-year period, its concomitant meaning changed several times. It first began as a food combination that American Jews ate in the late 1920s, then became a "Jewish food" in the 1930s. By the 1940s, it had reached iconic status and was used as a metonym for Jews. (*The Lowell Sun* in Massachusetts, for example, carried an article in 1948 about Grossinger's in the Catskills, reporting that, "The bagel-and-lox crowd was in stitches" ["Lox and Bagel Country"].[2]) In the 1940s it became a symbol of Jewish ethnicity that has continued until the present time ("bagels and lox Judaism") in which Jewish membership, though not religious observance, was implied. (In 2000, a Jewish author wrote: "My own Jewishness consists of a passionate belief in voting the straight Democratic ticket, fasting on Yom Kippur, eating bagels and lox—and doing no more" [Freedman 3].[3]) The bagels and lox combination also has a history (and meaning) beyond the Jewish community. In the 1960s, the combination began to be marketed outside Jewish ethnic enclaves and soon "crossed-over" to become another national food along with (Italian) pizza and (Mexican) tacos. Today it has been folded into the ultimate American melting-pot cuisine of twenty-first century "fusion" foods.[4]

Due to its multiple meanings, its iconic status in the Jewish community, and its changed physical properties to suit American consumers, it is not surprising that Jewish nostalgia has hidden the role played by the American food items; historical indifference has obscured how, over time, its component parts were modified. In order to clarify the historical record, I have taken seriously the sheer physicality of each food item that makes up the bagels and lox combination and examined the changing factors that influenced their manufacture (availability of ingredients, technological innovations, social factors that affected shape and taste) and their distribution (storage, transportation, marketing, and advertising). Thus, I will probe small but concrete data such as food prices, salt-curing processes, cream cheese fat-content, and the width of bagel holes. But, since food is never divorced from its context, I will also look at the symbolic meaning attached to this combination and the societal influences that shaped that meaning.

I contend that the bagels and lox combination was created at the end of the 1920s in New York City, which served as the vibrant center of Jewish life in the late nineteenth and early twentieth centuries.[5] By that time, *but not significantly before*, all of its component parts could be found within the Jewish community, were affordable by the second-generation children of immigrants, and appeared in the density and shape necessary for the combination to be assembled. Specifically, I will illustrate how the bagel began as a hard, dark European pretzel with an enormous hole and was transformed in America into a more chewable product, capable of being sliced, with a hole small enough to contain a *shmear* (spread) of *schmaltz* (rendered chicken fat), butter or cream cheese. I will detail how lox, an American product from the Pacific Northwest, eventually (though later than food historians state) made its way to the Jewish community of New York City. And I will present how and when cream cheese, a Yankee product, became a New York Jewish staple.

I will also explore the social and economic factors both within and without the Jewish community that influenced the creation of bagels and lox, fueled its popularity, and influenced its meaning. I suggest that the combination arose to display the rising economic status and increased Americanization of the second-generation Jewish immigrants of New York. Yet, unlike Anzia Yezierska's character in *Hungry Hearts* (1920) who exclaims after looking at the menu at a Lower East Side cafe: "Ain't there some American eating on the card?" (37–38) the bagels and lox combination was not a rejection of the food they had grown up eating. Rather, it involved an upscale exchange of familiar Jewish foods: lox for herring; cream cheese for butter or *schmaltz*. I suggest that this coalescence of ingredients was a perfect expression of the cultural pluralism that created American Judaism, that is, acculturation rather than assimilation. Just as the twentieth century rise of elaborate *bar* and *bat mitzvah* receptions and attention to gift-giving on Chanukah did not involve rejection of Jewish ritual and festival celebration but rather incorporated American material culture into already existent Jewish religious structures, so, too, the creation of the bagels and lox combination incorporated American foods and American forms of social status into already existent Jewish foodways.[6]

This exploration of the creation of bagels and lox not only augments food history and explores identity issues within the American Jewish community but also illuminates the sociological dynamics of immigration. It sheds light on the interplay between the forces of assimilation and accommodation that take place among all immigrant groups. In doing so, this examination highlights the tension between wholesale abandonment of ethnic markers, rituals, and practices by some new immigrants (as a way to blend quickly into the dominant culture) and a conservative "undertow" that insists on maintaining some elements of the "Old World." Such conservation cannot be ascribed simplistically to the generational divide between first generation immigrant parents, bewildered by their new society, and their children who are eager to embrace the dominant culture and shed all ties with their parents' world. Rather, as this history of the bagels and lox combination indicates, second generation immigrants have a complex "tug of war" between loyalty and identity. The creation of bagels, cream cheese and lox highlights this dialectic between the old world and a new one for Jewish immigrants and their children at the turn of the twentieth century as well as for other immigrant groups.[7]

THE TRANSFORMATION OF THE BAGEL

Appearing in an Eastern European document in 1501 and then mentioned specifically in connection with the Jewish community of Krakow in 1610, the bagel (from the Yiddish, *beygen*, to bend; Middle High German, *bügel*, ring; or the Austrian, *bügel*, a stirrup) was a ring-shaped bread made from flour, salt, water, yeast, and malt syrup. In Russia, it was most likely made from rye flour; in Poland and Ukraine, it was kneaded from a combination of rye and wheat. It was similar in shape to Italian *tarralli* and *brazatelle*, to Polish *obwarzanki*, and to Belarusian *smorgon baranki*. It had a hard crust (obtained by boiling

Figure 1: Warsaw Bagel Vendor, Forvertz, *23 October 1927.*

it first before baking) and a dense, "chewy" interior. Its texture was akin to a pretzel. Though there are legends as to the origin of its toroid shape (viz. so as to resemble a stirrup), it is more likely that the hole caused the dense interior to be cooked more evenly by the boiling water. The hole was also advantageous for removing bagels from boiling water and carrying or displaying them on a stick or on a string (Balinska letter; Balinska, *Bagel* 1–18, 20–21, 49; Cohen 38; Cooper 150; Ginsberg 8–9, 16; Goodman 91–92; Marks, *Encyclopedia* 35; Stampfer 178, n. 11, 193).[8] Two nineteenth century Polish engravings, a 1926 painting by a Polish Jewish artist, and a number of photos from Eastern Europe in the 1920s and 1930s, show that bagels were, originally, for the most part, the size of large bracelets—truly a hole surrounded by a bit of dough—with the hole approximately four and one-half inches in width and the bread around it about one-half inch in width (Balinksa, *Bagel* 53–57, 71–72; "People of a Thousand Towns").[9]

In the same way large, over-sized pretzels are eaten today—on their own or dipped in mustard—so too, bagels in Eastern Europe were eaten by themselves or dipped in butter or *schmaltz.* A Chasidic story, for example, from the mid-1700s, relates that the soul of Rabbi Avraham ("The Angel") would have left him when he was in an ecstatic state had not Rabbi Schneur Zalman of Liadi saved his life by forcing him to eat a piece of bagel with butter (Balinska letter; Cooper 151; Schneerson; see other examples in Stampfer 179).

Immigrant Jewish bakers brought over the bagel to America from Eastern Europe in the last decades of the nineteenth century. By 1895, bagel bakeries were found on New York's Lower East Side. In 1907, the first of the bagel baking unions was formed: International Beigel Bakers Union New York was followed by Bagel Bakers Union Local 338 in 1937 (Brenner 40–41; Goodman 91, 93, 98). It is likely that, initially, in America, the bagel was the same size and density as in Eastern Europe. An 1894 article on conditions in a New York bagel bakery, for example, identified the bagels as "pretzel biscuit" ("Bread and Filth").

When and how was the bagel transformed from a hard pretzel the size of a bracelet with a four and one-half inch hole to the soft, roll-like bagel of today with barely a half-inch hole? For most contemporary food historians, writers, and cookbook authors this has not been an issue. They have ignored the bagel's original large hole and pretzel-like consistency and assumed that the Eastern European bagel, though smaller than the super-sized bagel of today, always had a small hollow center. Though they assert that bagels were initially "chewier" than the softened bagels of today, they overlook its original hardness.

Moreover, they are not correct in assigning the softening process to the early 1960s (Balinska, *Bagel* 127–30; Feinsilver, "Bagel Shmear" 11–12; Levine; O'Neill; Sheraton, "Lost, Then Found"; Smith, *New York City* 168; Gabaccia 4; Young).

By the late 1920s, the bagel was transformed. Its hole had shrunk considerably and, though it still required "good teeth" to eat, the bagel was now softer than its Eastern European counterparts. An advertisement in a 1929 issue of the *Jewish Baker's Voice*, for example, shows an illustration of bagels with small holes. Even earlier, in 1926, Meyer Thompson (Tomoshowitz) (1891–1980), a Jewish baker from Hull, England, whose parents were bakers from Russia, created his second prototype for a bagel-making machine in Los Angeles. His newest invention, meant to duplicate the shape and size of hand-made bagels of his day, took two and one-half ounces of dough and formed it into a ring shape with an interior hole two and one-half inches in diameter. Such an emendation would have resulted, at the end of the cooking process, in a hole no larger than one-half inch in diameter, similar to most bagels today. Thus, by 1926 at the latest, the bagel had a hole small enough to prevent a *shmear* of *schmaltz*, butter or cream cheese from falling through it.[10]

Then, there was the bagel's density (not to mention the scant one-half-inch width of its ring) which would have made it impossible to split in order to serve as a platform for a *shmear*.[11] As the bagel's hole grew smaller, however, and its shape became more like a roll, its density changed as well. Changes began even earlier than 1963 when the soon-to-be ubiquitous bagel machine invented by Meyer Thompson's son Daniel called for more water to be added to the dough to prevent the machine from clogging. In the late 1950s, Lender's Bagels already produced a softer bagel by adding eggs and shortening to the dough. In 1951, an article in *Family Circle* suggested using bageles (sic) for an *hors d'oeuvres* recipe, stating: "Split these tender little triumphs in halves and then quarters" (Goodman 95, 97; Fox; Ginsberg and Berg 94; J. Nathan, *Jewish Cooking* 85; Thompson). In 1943, bagels and lox appeared on a Yiddish comedy sound recording, "Tyrone Shapiro (The Bronx Caballero)," and in 1937, the Jewish comedian Milton Berle professed his love for the combination (suggesting that one could slice the bagel by then) (Berle; "Tyrone Shapiro"; Howard).

The bagel's density probably softened even earlier, soon after the arrival of the Jewish immigrants to America beginning in the 1880s. Jewish bakers, who, in Eastern Europe, had been using primarily rye flour in the making of bread, now encountered an abundance of wheat flour in the US.[12] Accordingly, they began to introduce greater amounts of wheat flour (60–70 percent in the making of rye breads). Likely they did the same for bagels and created a rye and wheat mixture, which resulted in a softer product and a smaller hole.[13]

It was not, however, just the availability of these wheat flours that drove the change in the bagel's ingredients but consumer demands as well. By the turn of the twentieth century, social pressures pushed toward the consumption of softer (and whiter) foods. Settlement house workers encouraged immigrants to choose foods that conformed to Anglo-American ideals of whiteness. In the first decades of the twentieth century, Eastern European immigrants chose "white" not only as an expression of greater attention to hygiene and as a sign of embracing scientific progress but also as "an expression of responsible citizenship." Moreover, the Jewish embrace of white breads may be due not only to the allure of becoming acculturated Americans but, more specifically, the desire to be identified as *white* Americans. If, as Goldstein argues, second-generation Jewish immigrants by the 1920s were increasingly conscious of and concerned about their racial status in an America that defined people as "black" or "white," I suggest—given the (largely unconscious) symbolic function that food often plays—that the rejection of dark bread in favor of white, may have mirrored these concerns as well (Goldstein 121, 138–39, 145; Modan 116–30; Moss 90–94, 100–103). Finally, in contradistinction to the association of dark rye and pumpernickel breads with poverty, white bread and soft white rolls made with wheat symbolized status. Thus, by the late 1920s, it was estimated that white bread comprised 60 percent of the bread consumed in Jewish neighborhoods of New York (Balinska, *Bagel* 123–24; Bobrow-Strain 64–65, 96; Diner, *Hungering* 194; Evans 163; Gay 173–74; Gabaccia 61–62; Joselit 192; Merwin, *Pastrami on Rye* 36; Mintz 89; Stampfer 179; Tene 49; Young; Zanger 209).[14]

LOX ARRIVES IN NEW YORK

Lox (from the Yiddish, *laks*, salmon) originally referred to salt-cured salmon belly. Though Jews ate salted fish in Eastern Europe, it consisted of carp, pike, perch and trout for the wealthy and roach, chub and herring for the poor. Salmon was not part of their diet (Gostony 2–3; Edouard de Pomiane, cited in Roden 244–45; Wex 244–45). It was not until they arrived in America that Jews encountered lox, and even then, not until at least 1889, a decade after the first major waves of Eastern European immigration had begun.

In the eighteenth and mid-nineteenth centuries, Atlantic salmon was found in plentiful amounts in the rivers of New York, Maine, and Canada, and in the waters of Labrador and New Brunswick. By 1872, however, it had become expensive, commanding up to a dollar a pound. This increase in price related directly to availability—salmon appeared on the market only from April to August—and the fish had become scarce.[15] While the Pacific salmon remained abundant and available all year round, the costs of shipping it by boat to the East Coast which necessitated a trip around Cape Horn at the bottom of South America, rendered it, also, extremely expensive, affordable only by the wealthy.[16] With the completion of the Transcontinental Railroad in 1869, salmon, packed in ice, could travel directly across the US from Sacramento, California to the East Coast, but the expense of ice refrigeration kept shipping quantities small (see below). Moreover, by this time, there was a scarcity of salmon in the Sacramento River as a result of gold mining operations, begun in 1848, that dammed its waters, clogged them with slurry, and filled them with toxic mercury (used for ore refinement).

Salmon filled the Pacific waters and rivers of Oregon and Washington but no rail line existed to connect them with the East Coast. A line did not open until 1888 when the Northern Pacific Railway completed its transcontinental line that linked Puget Sound (Washington), a key area for salmon fishing, to St. Paul, Minnesota and, from there, eastward. By 1889, salmon in enormous quantities began to be shipped from the West Coast. Most of it was chopped into pieces, packed in cans, and then steam-cooked before shipping.[17]

Some of the Pacific salmon, however, was shipped whole and uncooked for later consumption. Chinook (King) salmon was primarily used, due to its size that made handling easier.[18] These salmon were carefully cleaned, split open, deboned, and washed. Then, since fish are particularly susceptible to spoiling when exposed to oxygen, "hard" salt curing was employed which prevented bacteria from growing: the salmon were placed in layers in a tank, with twelve–fifteen pounds of salt per one hundred pounds of fish sprinkled over each layer. The tank was then filled with a 90 percent salt brine. After one week, the salmon were removed from the tank and packed in barrels of two-hundred-pound lots which were filled with a new brine solution before being shipped.[19]

Though ice refrigeration for food shipping had already been in development since the late 1860s, the West Coast fishing companies slowly adopted it as a replacement for salt-curing because of the expense involved. Capital expenditures for icing stations and ice-making factories (using steam-driven pistons to compress ammonia, thus freezing the surrounding water) were needed all along the rail route to replenish the melted ice, and the railroads charged higher shipping fees for the "reefers" (insulated railroad cars) that were more expensive to build and maintain than the standard box cars. In addition, the dissolved salts in the salmon's flesh from its salt water habitat, meant, unlike other foods that were frozen and shipped, that it would not freeze at 32° Fahrenheit. Decomposition occurred unless it was frozen below 15°, requiring even more ice, thus adding to the cost (Cobb 136–38; Danes-Wingett 1–3, 6; Gantz 50–55; Gosnell 377–78, 386; Jensen 23–24; Reese 88–92; Stampfer 180).

By the early 1900s, the development of cold storage and the railroad "icing chain" was sufficiently developed for the West Coast fisheries to introduce "mild" salt-curing. In this curing process, the salmon were packed in tierces (large wooden forty-two gallon casks), each of which held 800 to 825 pounds of salmon. They were layered with half the amount of salt used for hard curing—6.6 pounds per one humdred pounds of fish—and the salmon held for twenty to ninety days in cold storage before being repacked in brine for shipping (Cobb 129–32; Freeman 109, 127–28; Grader 1–2; United States Tariff Commission 59).

Initially, most of the salt-cured salmon was not shipped to the East Coast for Jewish immigrant consumption but for export to European markets via New York's Atlantic port. Some tierces were delivered to New York smokeries before being shipped overseas; others remained in the brine barrels. A smaller amount of salmon arriving from the Northwest was delivered to fish brokers in New York who distributed them to wholesale markets for sale to hotels, restaurants, and retail fish stores.[20] The salmon were removed from the barrels, then washed and soaked to reduce their salt composition from 19 percent to 2 percent. At some point after 1889, a market developed in the New York Jewish community for salt-cured salmon and for salt-cured salmon that had been smoked upon its arrival (Cobb 129–33, 146; Grader 2).[21]

Though salmon became more plentiful, it still strained immigrant budgets, which is why the lower-cost herring continued to be consumed in large quantities on the Lower East Side. Lox, at between seven to nine cents for a quarter pound in the 1920s, was only a little less expensive than a quarter pound of chicken or beef rib roast (9.5 cents). When immigrant families bought it, they did so usually in small quantities of *halbe fiertel*, half of a quarter (that is, two thin strips of lox weighing a total of two ounces), then divided it up further among family members. They ate these small strips just as they had eaten salt-cured herring in Eastern Europe: placed on dark bread spread with butter or *schmaltz*. They also mixed small pieces into sour cream, and fried, poached, or grilled the less expensive lox trimmings (called *fliegelen*, wings), which came mostly from the fins and tails.[22]

CREAM CHEESE ENTERS THE LOWER EAST SIDE

While Jews in Eastern Europe who were well-to-do had milk regularly and those who had some income could purchase milk from a dairyman to occasionally supplement their daily diet of bread, potatoes, onions, and herring, milk seems to have been a relatively scarce item for the masses of poverty-stricken Jews in the Russian Empire during the nineteenth century and early twentieth centuries. This limited access was especially true in the winter when forage was buried in snow and limited fodder was available. Around 1900, for example, Shmul Chaim Levi of Kaluszyn, Poland, handed out cash to the needy to buy milk, and as late as 1933, David Shapira returned to his *shtetl* of Horodok, Poland and distributed money to the community and served milk to the children. Yet, certain communities did have access to milk. Accounts of Jewish village life, especially in Lithuania, sometimes mention ownership of a cow or goat and consumption of sour milk, butter, sour and sweet cream, farmers cheese and pot cheese (Ben-Dov; Cooper 151–54, 159–61; Deutsch and Saks 13–14; Diner, *Hungering* 161–63; Heinze 35; Kirshenblatt-Gimblett; National Center for Jewish Film; Pasklinksi 259; O. Schwartz 71; Tene 48; Wex 221; Zborowski and Herzog 369, 391). However, while the availability or scarcity of milk was not uniform throughout Eastern European communities, there is consensus that cream cheese was not being produced nor consumed. Though for decades, the Yiddish word, *shmear*, in America, has been associated with cream cheese, it was originally used in Eastern Europe in connection with butter or had the general meaning of smearing or greasing (Philologos). Edourd de Pomiane's 1929 collection of Polish Jewish recipes, *Cuisine Juive: Ghettos Modernes*, contained dairy ingredients such as double cream, butter, sour cream, and cottage cheese but no cream cheese. A 1938 vegetarian cookbook from Vilna, Lithuania, lists Swiss and farmer cheese, sour and heavy cream but not cream cheese for its four hundred recipes (Lewando; de Pomiane).

As I have shown elsewhere, cream cheese was actually developed in the United States. Dutch and English settlers brought early recipes for cream cheese, made by combining milk and cream, to America. By the early 1800s dairy farmers in and around the Philadelphia area produced it in small quantities. Around 1875, thanks to advances in rail transportation, steam engine technology, and commercial ice production, an upstate New York dairy farmer, William Lawrence, began to mass-manufacture cream cheese. By 1880, thanks to Lawrence's distributor, Alvah Reynolds, the cream cheese had acquired a brand name—Philadelphia—and was delivered to food emporia throughout New York City. By 1903, at least ten competing cream cheese brands existed in New York (Marx, "Philadelphia®"; Marx, "Days Had Come"). But while the introduction of cream cheese to the New York grocery trade occurred at exactly the time of the Jewish Eastern European arrival to the US, the Jewish immigrant community did not, at first, consume this cheese. Cream cheese was a fancy, expensive cheese, far beyond their means. In 1889, a pound of Muenster sold for thirteen cents, Parmesan for twenty-three cents, while cream cheese cost thirty cents. In 1893, domestic cheese went for fifteen cents a pound, while cream cheese cost twenty-five cents; and in 1909, cottage cheese retailed for twenty cents a pound, while cream cheese went up to forty cents ("Of Interest"; Dahlberg 107; Marx, "Days Had Come" 184; Publow 4, 9–10).

Thus, it was not until 1918 that the first advertisements for cream cheese (Yankee Cream Cheese) made their appearance in the Yiddish press. Ads for Blue Bird and Philadelphia Cream Cheese followed these in 1920 (Delaware Cheese Co. Inc.; Heinze 158–59; Louis Kadans, "Yankee Cream Cheese," 19 Nov. 1918; Louis Kadans, "Yankee Cream Cheese: A Taste of Eden!"; Phenix, "Philadelphia Cream Cheese," 7 April 1920).[23] In 1923, Breakstone Bros.—started by Joseph and Isaac Bregshtein, who had operated in New York City since 1897 as dairy commission merchants and since 1906 as dairy product manufacturers—began producing Breakstone's Downsville Cream Cheese in five pound loaves for sale to retail grocers (Breakstone Bros., "Downsville Cream Cheese," 6 Feb. 1924; "Alleged $40,000 Thief"; Breakstone Bros., Cream cheese box; "Breakstone Bros."; Breakstone Bros., Inc., of New York, NY; State of New York Dept. of Agriculture 93). Though cream cheese, since 1880, had been manufactured, wrapped, and sold in small, three-ounce packages, and although individually wrapped products replaced bulk items in grocery stores, Breakstone Bros., clearly with their eye on limited budgets, bulk-packaged this cheese for the retail grocer to cut up into small amounts for the customer.[24]

Like the advertisements from the dairy companies that preceded them, Breakstone Bros., too, praised the quality, nutritious benefits, and taste of their product. But unlike the serving suggestions put forth in Yankee and Philadelphia cream cheese ads—"Try it with crackers or bread"; "Mix it into scrambled eggs"; "Cut out a ripe, cold tomato. Fill it with Philadelphia cream cheese"—Breakstone also pitched their product specifically to the Jewish consumer. Their ads suggested that cream cheese could be substituted for the soft white cheeses used in familiar Jewish recipes. A 1924 ad stated, "Cheese Kreplach. Everyone loves it. But you will love it even more when it's filled with Breakstone's Downsville Cream Cheese." A 1927 ad read, "Your Hamentaschen Will Be Delicious if you fill them with Breakstone's Downsville Cream Cheese." To aid in this substitution process, Breakstone Bros. advertisements proclaimed that their cheese was strictly kosher (Breakstone Bros., "Downsville Cream Cheese," 2 June 1925, 17 June 1925, 5 Aug. 1925, and 16 March 1927; Gay 171–72; Louis Kadans, "Yankee Cream Cheese," 1 Dec. 1918; Phenix, "Philadelphia Cream Cheese," *23* July 1920, 17 Aug. 1921, and 15 Nov. 1922).[25]

Figure 2: Forvertz, *January 22, 1926.*

"Mothers! Don't Speculate With the Health of Your Children! . . . We are sure that the Jewish mother doesn't want to hold back a few cents when it has to do with the health of her entire family."

Cheesecake provides an example of their success in substituting cream cheese for familiar Jewish recipes. Though usually made with curd cheese, a 1925 Breakstone's ad proposed the substitution: "Cheesecake has a wonderful taste . . . when you make it with Breakstone's Downsville Cream Cheese. Try it one time and you will agree that you have not yet eaten such a good cheese cake in your life." In the late 1920s, Arnold Reuben, a delicatessen owner in New York, began using Breakstone's cream cheese in his cheesecakes instead of curd cheese and won a gold medal at the 1929 World's Fair in Spain for his recipe. Cream cheese soon became the key ingredient in "New York cheesecake."[26]

In addition to substituting cream cheese for the soft, white cheese used in Jewish recipes, Breakstone Bros. also suggested using it to *shmear* on rye bread in place of *schmaltz* and butter, which, heretofore, had been utilized both in Eastern Europe and in America (Federman 21; Kisseloff 41).[27] (The decrease in popularity of *schmaltz* certainly aided their efforts. By 1912, Crisco began replacing *schmaltz* as a kosher and *pareve* cooking fat made from hydrogenized cottonseed oil; then, in 1924, Nyafat, made from coconut oil flavored with onion, rose in popularity.)[28] A 1924 ad for their cream cheese stated, "It has a fine buttery taste . . . it melts in your mouth like fine, fresh farm butter!" A 1925 ad proclaims, "Give your children bread spread with Breakstone's Downsville Cream Cheese" (Breakstone Bros., "Give Your Children Bread," 3 Dec. 1925; Breakstone Bros., "It Has a Fine Buttery Taste!" 20 Feb. 1924).

Breakstone's brand name recognition within the Jewish community, targeted marketing to the Jewish consumer, and extensive distribution network to New York grocers—established over a twenty-five-year period—was, I will submit, the main reason for the entry of cream cheese into the New York Jewish community by the late 1920s (Harry Breakstone interview; Breakstone Bros. Bronx Branch, Inc.; "David Breakstone"; Denker 82; "Fire in Wallabout Market"; C. C. Miller 244; "New Incorporations"; R. L. Polk & Co.; The Trow City Directory Co. [1899, 1900, 1902]). However, some of their success was also due to the taste and structure of this new product. Whereas most cream cheeses in this period consisted of 26 percent milk fat, Breakstone's cream cheese contained over 37 percent, which resulted in a creamy, rich "mouthfeel" (Breakstone Bros., "Downsville Cream Cheese," 13 Feb. 1924; Breakstone Bros. Cream cheese box, 5 lb.; Dahlberg 106; "Green Vegetables"; Lundstedt 243; McCann). Moreover, once cream cheese had entered the Jewish community, it would not have taken long to discover that it served as a good foil to the salt-cured lox shipped from the West Coast and that its stiffer texture allowed it to be spread over a bagel hole.[29]

Finally, there was the issue of economics. Though cream cheese in 1925 was still relatively expensive (forty-nine cents a pound, equivalent to a shopping cart containing a quart of milk, one pound of beans, one pound of onions, one pound of rice, and two pounds of potatoes) it was slightly less expensive than butter (over fifty-three cents a pound).[30] Accordingly, Breakstone ads touted that fact: "It contains so much butter fat that you will save on butter." Also, by the 1920s, the income of second-generation Jewish immigrant children who had then come of age had risen. Cream cheese, especially when purchased in smaller amounts, would have been affordable for them (Breakstone Bros., "Cheese Kreplach"; Breakstone Bros., "Tuviya the Dairyman Says"; Levenstein 175).

It should be noted, that in the mid-1920s, when Breakstone Bros. suggested that their cream cheese be used as a substitute for butter and *schmaltz*, all their ads stated it was to be *shmeared* on bread not on bagels (Breakstone Bros., "It Has a Fine Buttery Taste!"; Breakstone Bros., "Policeman"; Breakstone Bros., "Our Reputation"). Accounts of Jewish life on the Lower East Side relate that rye and black bread (not bagels) were spread with garlic and butter or with *schmaltz*; pickled herring was eaten with bread and butter. A writer on kosher restaurants noted in 1929, somewhat tongue in cheek, that rye bread was important on the Lower East Side because it could be used as a plate (Gay 170; Kisselhof 41; Glass; Zara 80). It was the practical base for spreads until the bagels and lox combination was created.

EATING UP

By the late 1920s, all the components of the bagels and lox combination were in place within the New York Jewish community. Cream cheese, an American food, was distributed throughout the Lower East Side by 1924 and was advertised as a replacement for butter. The bagel, by 1926 (and probably before), had become softer, and its hole smaller, allowing each sliced half to serve as a platform for a *schmear*. Second generation immigrants could afford lox in larger amounts (Breakstone Bros., "Cream Cheese With Lox").[31] I suggest that the uptown theater-district kosher-style delicatessens were the location where these components were brought together.

As Merwin has noted, the delicatessen was a place of Jewish safety and comfort, a perfect example of Oldenburg's "third place," where Jews "could eat with their hands, talk with their mouths full, fill their bellies, and enjoy the pleasure of each other's company in a raucous and convivial setting" (*Pastrami on Rye* 12).[32] But the kosher-*style* delicatessen served symbolic functions as well. While traditional Jewish boundaries separating meat and milk had been reinforced in New York, respectively, by the kosher deli and the appetizing store, the kosher-style deli that offered milk and meat foods together very publically rejected that tradition. (For example, Lindy's served The Tongue Temptation, a sandwich containing both tongue and Swiss cheese.) Moreover, I would suggest that the introduction of dairy into the delicatessen realm of meat mirrored the increased entry of New York women into the social domain of men that took place at this time.[33] Thus, it was also a symbolic rejection of traditional Jewish boundaries between the sexes.[34] The kosher-style deli did not, however, reject Jewish identity *in toto*—after all, it was a Jewish space—but rather was a setting in which familiar Jewish foods were presented along with new American foods and social elements. The kosher-style deli brought together American urban culture *and* immigrant Jewish culture. It reflected the dynamic tensions between the ethnic community that bound the second-generation immigrants and the enticements of America that urged them further away from their roots (Heinze 5; Dash Moore 4–5, 11; Rosenbaum 257–58).

The location of these kosher-style delis was important as well. They were in the theater district, which, during the 1920s, was filled with the glamour of celebrity producers, singers, dancers, comedians, actors, professional gamblers and notorious gangsters, many of whom were Jewish. Walter Winchell and other columnists transmitted to millions over the radio and in tabloids such as the *Daily News*, the *Daily Mirror*, and *Evening Graphic* "the nightlife, the in-jokes, the show-business scuttlebutt . . . the lingo of Broadway." The theatre district kosher-style delis not only became the social center for many of Broadway's denizens but became places where socially-aspiring second-generation immigrants could go to mingle with the successful or at least share the same space with them. These Broadway delis "flattered Jewish social and economic aspirations."[35] They did so, not just by providing a shared space with the famous and successful but also, symbolically, by the food that they served. These delicatessens became sites (and sights) for conspicuous consumption, specifically of meat—a sign for the immigrants and their children of economic status—in the form of overstuffed sandwiches of pastrami and corned beef (Diner, *Hungering* 161–64, 179–80).[36]

The consumption of sandwiches was a signature feature of the 1920s. In the years following Prohibition, there was a great expansion in restaurants catering to lunch-hour workers. The trade journal *Mogen Dovid Delicatessen Magazine* reported in 1932 that the sandwich trade had increased 215 percent since 1920. Though the dates vary in which Arnold Reuben claimed to have first created his eponymous sandwich (a jumbo concoction of corned beef, sauerkraut, and melted Swiss on pumpernickel bread spread with Russian dressing), it is clear that by 1922, he served overstuffed sandwiches named after celebrities who gathered in his kosher-style deli. Leo Linderman, the owner of Lindy's delicatessen, also began serving overstuffed specialty sandwiches in the 1920s.[37] By 1926, there was said to be over 5,000 shops in New York City that specialized in serving over 946 different kinds of sandwiches.[38] The sandwiches were expensive: $1.25 in 1926. For that amount, one could buy a pound of sirloin steak, a dozen eggs, a pound of flour and a quart of milk at the grocery store or have a full dinner and show at a cabaret. But that was exactly the point. These expensive smoked and pickled meats, consumed in huge amounts, were a symbolic luxury, a reminder that the second generation now crossed the socio-economic boundaries that had, initially, separated them as poor immigrants on the Lower East Side from native-born Americans. If, as Wilkes suggests, cuisine is a matter of public display and performance, then these kosher-style delis, located in the midst of the stage world, served as the logical setting (versus the private space of home) for the presentation and consumption of overstuffed foods, a visible sign that they had "made it" in America.[39]

Figure 3: Reuben's Restaurant Menu, 23 April 1922. Courtesy, Henry Voigt, The Henry Voigt Collection of American Menus.

Reuben's Famous Sandwiches

Imported Unsalted Malossal Caviar	$2.00	Roast Virginia Ham	$ .40
Club a la Reuben	1.00	Roast Beef	.40
Reuben's Special	.85	Prime Rib of Beef	.65
Reuben's Paradise	.85	Spiced Beef	.35
Ina Claire Special	.85	Liver Wurst	.35
Francine Larrimore Special	.85	Liver Wurst and Bermuda Onions	.50
Gladys Feldman Special	.85	Home Boiled Ham	.35
Tartar Sandwich a la Al. Jolson	1.00	Home Boiled Tongue	.40
Peggy Joyce Special	.85	Brisket Corned Beef	.35
Reuben's Steak Sandwich	1.00	Salami	.35
Reuben's Superior	.90	Roast Pork	.40
Reuben's Tongue Delite	.65	Imported Swiss Cheese	.35
Marjorie Rambeau Special	.85	Rocquefort Cheese	.50
Marillyn Miller Special	.85	Cream Cheese and Bar le Duc	.50
Lilyan Tashman Special	.75	American Cheese	.35
Fay Marbe Special	.75	Camembert Cheese	.50
Reuben's Turkey Sandwich, Russian Dressing	.60	Lake Sturgeon	.65
Roast Virginia Ham and Imported Swiss Cheese	.65	Nova Scotia Salmon	.50
Turkey and Virginia Ham	.75	Anchovy Paste	.40
Chicken Salad, Russian Dressing	.50	Sardellan Butter	.40
		Sardine	.60

Virginia Ham and Egg Sandwich .75

One food writer has noted that, after World War II, when smoked fish was expensive, "appetizing was a way for the newly affluent to show off their success. . . . Everyone on line behind you or around you could hear what you ordered" (A. Schwartz 157). I would suggest that such status consciousness about fish was already being proclaimed more than a decade earlier. In the second half of the 1920s, in the midst of the theater-district kosher-style delis that offered dairy, fish and meat products, a new, expensive sandwich concoction was also served alongside sandwiches stacked high with deli meat.[40] It consisted of a sliced bagel *shmeared* not with butter (or *schmaltz*) but with cream cheese, a high-status product. Then, just like the oversized deli sandwiches around it, the bagel was stuffed with several times the amount of lox that they had eaten as children. The contrast between the "poor" food of their youth and the upscale food in copious amounts that was now on their plate could not have been clearer to them and to others.[41]

Various theories on the origin of bagels and lox, repeatedly quoted in cook books, Internet sites, and food encyclopedias, though incorrect, retain, nonetheless, the historical memory that the creation of the combination was linked with Broadway stars and entertainers. These include the theories that Al Jolson and other entertainers, as hosts of the Kraft Music Hall radio show, put the combination together around 1933 after being instructed by Kraft to weave mention of their dairy products into the show.[42] Another suggests that Al Jolson made the combination popular with a song from the 1930s, called "Bagels and Yox."[43]

While the bagels and lox combination displayed the rising economic status and increased Americanization of the second generation immigrants, it also demarcated, for some, the limits of their assimilation in that it did not consist of "outside" food, such as bacon or ham. The impetus behind their consumption of the bagels and lox combination was not necessarily to reject the fare of their youth (Abusch-Magder 53, 76; Dash Moore 75; Fishman 9–11; Kraut 410, 417; Lem 96–97; Weber 3).[44] For example, Marks suggested that it was a kosher substitution for the brunch classic Eggs Benedict during the 1930s in which bagel, lox, and cream cheese replaced English muffin, ham, and hollandaise sauce (Marks, *Encyclopedia* 36.). Though he affirms my contention that rejection was not at work, here, I do not think that this theory is correct: why substitute every ingredient when only the ham would need replacing? Also, brunch, a late Sunday morning meal, did not become part of American Jewish foodways until the late 1940s, long after the establishment of the bagels and lox combination.[45]

Another theory on the origin of the combination suggests that though outright rejection was not at work, symbolic rejection played the determining role. Regelson proposed that bagels and lox eaten on Sunday mornings in the 1940s was a figurative transgression of kosher restrictions: red lox resembling ham (meat) was combined with cream cheese (dairy) (Regelson). His social setting for this theory, however, is not correct. First, the bagels and lox combination was in existence for over ten years before this proposed date. Second, as I note, above, Jews were not sitting down to brunch until the *end* of the 1940s.[46] Third, this proposed 1940s date for the creation of the combination seems quite late for Jewish symbolic food rejection, since the kosher-style delis had already, for two decades, been providing a space in which the kosher laws were both actually and symbolically transgressed, and since Chinese food containing actual (not symbolic) pork and non-kosher meat had been a staple in the Jewish community for previous decades, as well.[47]

No, the creation of bagels and lox was not driven by kosher substitution nor symbolic rejection but rather by aspirational exchange. Second-generation immigrants replaced the "poor" food and the small amounts of their childhoods with large quantities of upscale delicacies. The front cover of the story of Russ & Daughters appetizing store perhaps illustrates this exchange best. Underneath its title "Reflections and Recipes from the House that Herring Built" one finds not a picture of herring but rather an oversized bagel and cream cheese, piled high with lox. In the same way that, traditionally, the story of the Israelites' exodus from Egypt, told at the Passover table, "begins with degradation and ends in exaltation," so, too, the immigrant Jews began with dark rye bread, butter, and herring, and their children ended with bagels, cream cheese, and lox. By the end of the 1920s, bagels and lox offered a conspicuous sign, for the second-generation immigrant Jews of New York, that they had truly "arrived" in the American Promised Land (Federman, *Russ and Daughters*; Merwin, *In Their Own Image* 10; *Mishnah Pesachim* 10:4).[48]

******

ACKNOWLEDGEMENTS

My thanks to the library staff at Hebrew Union College-Jewish Institute of Religion, Los Angeles; Eric Bryon, Ellis Island Immigration Museum, New York, for his discography help; Michael Dicianna at the Oregon State University Special Collections and Archive Research Center for his assistance in unearthing obscure data about salmon processing; Charles Ducat, Thompson Bagel Machine Mfg. Corp., for sharing his knowledge of bagel production; Miriam Koral, California Institute for Yiddish Culture and Language, for her invaluable aid in translating Yiddish cream cheese ads; and the countermen of Nate 'n Al Delicatessen in Los Angeles and the late Carnegie Deli of New York, for their patience and good humor in weighing out for me various proportions of thinly sliced lox, and thickly sliced corned beef.

Notes

1. For an introduction to foodways, see Diner (*Hungering* 3–9).
2. The bagel, as a discrete food item, was also employed as a synonym for Jews. See, for example, the term "Bagel Beach" as used to describe the collection of Jewish summer cottages in Bradley Beach, New Jersey and in Milford, Connecticut (Dion; Navarra 24). For a discussion of bagels as an iconic food, see Stampfer (187–89).
3. See also Halter (6–7); Joselit (171); Roth (69): "We were bagels-and-lox secular Jews, who never talked religion or faith, and rarely went to temple. . . ." For details of symbolic ethnicity, see Gans (1–20).
4. For examples of the bagel as a fusion food, such as the pizza bagel, the St. Patrick's Day green bagel, bagel chips, and baked flour tortillas *shmeared* with chipotle crème fraiche and topped with tequila cured salmon, see Batt (28–29); Beatrice and Ira Henry Freeman; Feinsilver ("Bagel Shmear" 10–11); and Stacy's Bagel Chips. It has also become English slang: "a bagel" can refer to a TV show that is lacking something and "getting the bagel" is a tennis term for losing a set 6–0 (Belasco 1–29; Balinska 156–76; Feinsilver, "Bagel Shmear" 9; Gabaccia 2, 4–5; Breskin, Brown and Otieno).
5. Though here I focus on the origins of the bagels and lox combination in the United States, specifically in New York City, I am mindful that both bagels and lox have a developmental history in both England and Canada as well. As far as other American Jewish urban centers are concerned, I would hold that the appearance of bagels and lox in those cities followed its original creation in New York. For example, the majority of kosher-style delicatessens that, I contend in this article, were the primary vehicle for the popularization of the combination, were established in Los Angeles by Jewish transplants from the New York area. In addition, Boyle Heights, the ethnic enclave of the Los Angeles Jewish community, did not begin to arise until the late 1920s, by which time the combination had already been established in New York. A 1932 Jewish cookbook from Portland in the Pacific Northwest—the center of salmon fishing—has no mention of bagels and lox and instead presents a sandwich recipe for rye bread, cream cheese and sardines (Council of Jewish Women 418; Luce; Merwin, *Pastrami on Rye* 102–04; Sadow 1–2, 3–9; Weber 175–76).
6. For detailed examples of Jewish Eastern European immigrants incorporating American material culture see Joselit, and Heinze.
7. For an in-depth examination of food and immigrant identity, see Gabaccia, and Diner, *Hungering*.
8. Though its spelling and pronunciation is rendered in various ways (*bajgele*, *bajgiel*, *beigel*, *beygl*), I use the "Americanized" spelling of bagel throughout this article.
9. There have been several attempts to reconstruct the bagel's volume and weight in the nineteenth century by applying *halakhic* definitions of what amount of bread

constitutes a meal—thus requiring a concluding blessing—to the Yiddish saying: "One is only satisfied from the third bagel" (Stampfer 178–79; Wex 227–28). However, determining the exact measurement from just one folk saying is difficult, especially given differences among the legal authorities in defining the minimum (*kazayit*) amount of food that constitutes a meal (*shiur seudah*) ("Pat Haba Bikisnin"; Slifkin 3, 23). At best, it can be said that this folk saying suggests that bagels were smaller (in volume) than they are today.

10. It is likely, however, since Meyer's first prototype was built around 1920, that the bagel had changed shape by then. Though his first prototype was built in Winnipeg, Canada, and the second prototype in Los Angeles, by 1919, Thompson had spent time on the East Coast, where his brother lived ("Meyer Thompson," *U. S. Border Crossings*; "Meyer Thompson," *U. S. Naturalization Record Indexes*; "Meyer Thompson," *U. S., Social Security Death Index*; Ducat interview; Ginsberg and Berg 98; *Jewish Baker's Voice*; Thompson; "Abram Thompson," *1891 England Census*; "Abraham Thompson," *1901 England Census*).
11. Perhaps this is also why, in Eastern Europe, the bialy was never sliced, instead smeared on either its top or bottom with butter or soft cheese (Sheraton, *Bialy Eaters* 51, 100).
12. Though wheat and wheat-rye products were not unknown in the Russian Empire—exports from the US began arriving in the 1850s and wheat began to be planted in Ukrainian fields—the amount of wheat per week consumed by an average inhabitant in Poland appears to have been small. While in 1866, US farmers produced forty pounds of rye for every American, by 1900 production had dropped to twenty pounds due to 49.2 million acres of US prairie land used to grow wheat (Balinska, *Bagel* 50; Ginsberg 16–17; Ginsberg and Berg 56–57; Jacob 290–98; Wex 219–21).
13. The elastic gluten strands in high-gluten wheat flour—which tighten during mixing and shaping—subsequently relax during the proofing (resting) process before boiling. Thus, while a gluten-free rye bagel formed with a five inch hole retains that hole size, the five inch hole of a wheat bagel expands, resulting in a smaller (two-inch) hole. There may be other factors that also played a role in the bagel hole's diminishment. One possibility is that the sheer quantity of inexpensive flour that became available to the Jewish immigrant bakers in America led to the "bulking up" of the bagel, resulting in more surface, less hole. A second possibility is that increased consumer demands fueled by the teeming Jewish population of the Lower East Side were placed upon a small, tightly-controlled number of Jewish bagel bakers. This may have led to the creation of smaller bagels (and, hence, smaller holes) so to fit more in boiling pots and baking ovens (Beitcher interview; Ginsberg 79–81, 93–96; Ginsberg and Berg 57–60; Wex 221–22).
14. Though the increase of wheat flour was now lightening dark rye breads, why did the whitening and softening process not proceed further? Why did corned beef

not end up on white bread but continued, up to the present time, to pair with rye? Already, in 1937, an advertisement for Levy's rye bread that appeared in *Mogen Dovid Delicatessen Magazine* called attention to this phenomenon. Wilk has labeled this "The Mintz Paradox," quoting a line by the food historian, Sidney Mintz: "We do not understand at all well why it can be claimed both that people cling tenaciously to familiar old foods, yet readily replace some of them with others" (Mintz 24; "Things You Never Hear" 10; Wilk, "Paradoxes of Jews" 232).

15. By 1929 salmon were all but exterminated on the Atlantic Coast of the United States (Clift 19, 22; Coates 69; Filipini 8–10; Netboy, *Atlantic Salmon* 322–31; United States Tariff Commission 4).
16. Compare the circa 1872 salmon yield from the Penobscot River in Maine—8,000 fish—with the 1870 yield from the Columbia river in Oregon—almost two million pounds. In 1890, the catch on the Pacific Coast was estimated to be more than ten million salmon (Clift 22; Freeman 109; Jensen 1, 13–14). Given the plentitude of salmon, consumers on the West Coast paid much less for salmon. In 1853, salmon caught on the Sacramento River in California and shipped directly to San Francisco was only two cents a pound (Netboy, *Columbia River Salmon* 19–20; "Sacramento Salmon Fisheries" 100).
17. Since they swam in schools and each catch resulted in thousands of fish, not only did canning become a fast way of processing the fish, but it also preserved the fish for long periods of time, eliminated the cost of ice refrigeration, and benefitted consumers who, upon opening the can, now had cooked fish immediately available to eat (Clift 22; Freeman 118; Jensen 25–28; Netboy, *Columbia River Salmon*, 21, 23–24; Solnit 100–03). For a detailed look at the history of salmon canning, see O'Bannon, and Mink (51–70). It is interesting to note that an American Jewish scholar, around the turn of the nineteenth century, in answering a question as to the kosher status of salmon and lox, refers to canned salmon (Eisenstein 353). I thank Shaul Stampfer for bringing this source to my attention.
18. Salmon fisheries also packed salmon bellies separately but, since they took more time to cut and the rest of the fish was thrown away, thus causing a waste of choice product, fewer barrels of belly were produced than of the whole fish. In 1902, for example, while Alaskan fisheries packed over 30,384 (800 lb.) barrels of whole salmon, only 328 barrels of salmon bellies were produced. The fact that lox trimmings (from the fins and tails) were consumed by the Jewish immigrants of New York (see below) suggests that they had access to the whole salmon and not just its belly (Cobb 7–8, 132–34, 180; United States Tariff Commission 65).
19. If the salmon were not split open and washed, enzymes in their stomachs continued the process of breaking down undigested food along with their flesh, resulting in "belly burn," which disfigured the fish. The salmon was preserved through curing; the salt, through osmosis, drew water out from the salmons' cell walls. Some of

that water, saturated with salt, then returned to the cells, coagulating the salmons' proteins, which made it difficult for bacteria to flourish and start the process of decomposition (Cobb 133; Freeman 127; Grader 1–2; Jensen 21; Mink 34).

20. Of the $535,000 worth of non-canned shipments of salmon to Europe in 1900, $347,000 worth was shipped from Atlantic ports, most of it from New York (Coates 72; Cobb 195, 199; Gantz 59–61; Mink 49–50; United States Tariff Commission 60, 62).
21. A detailed study of Jewish involvement in brokerage and retail distribution of lox, as well as in the cold-smoking of lox at the turn of the twentieth century, has yet to be written. See "At H. Forman & Son"; DeLoach (259–60); *Pacific Fisherman* issues, beginning in 1903; Roden (63); and "Appetizing Stores." Atlantic Salmon was also available to the New York Jewish community, though in much smaller quantities. Like the Pacific salmon, it was salted and packed in tierces. A 1922 menu from Reuben's Restaurant, for example, lists a Nova Scotia salmon sandwich. By the second half of the twentieth century, however, the origins of salmon sold in delicatessens became obscured, as all cold-smoked lox, regardless of its source, was called Nova (Knight 32; Marks, *Encyclopedia* 31; "Menu," Reuben's Restaurant).
22. By 1930, smoked lox came up to twenty cents a pound (Bittman; Braun 24–25; Federman 25, 138; Gabaccia 46; Kinetz; Marks, *Encyclopedia* 370–71; A Schwartz 154; "Fair Price List" 14; "1920's Food and Groceries Prices"). For herring consumption, see Diner (*Hungering* 161–63, 186, 199); Joselit (202); Netboy, *Columbia River Salmon* (28); Wasserman (157).
23. Though Florence Greenbaum's *The International Jewish Cookbook* (1919) contained a recipe for cream cheese, it described soft, white cheese with butter mixed in, a far cry from the cream cheeses in the advertisements (Greenbaum 202).
24. They were not the only ones to do so. A 1924 ad for their cheese stated: "Once they used to sell cream cheese only in little closed packages. Therefore, one could immediately see what sort of cheese this is and who made this cheese. But today, cream cheese is sold also loose, by the pound, so that the Jewish grocer man and the Jewish homemaker need to be more careful" (Breakstone Bros., "Remember Our Label"; Hine 70–71, 81–82, 125; Marx, "Philadelphia®" 186, 188–89; Phenix, "Always Fresh").
25. Philadelphia cream cheese ads placed in the *Forvertz* seem to be Yiddish translations of previous ads placed in the English language press (Phenix, "Philadelphia Cream Cheese Hawaiian Salad").
26. Most food histories cite Reuben's claim and the claim of his son, Arnold Reuben, Jr., that Reuben was the first, in 1928/29, to utilize cream cheese instead of curd cheese in cheesecake. While Arnold Reuben may be given credit for the popularization of this cheesecake using Breakstone's cream cheese, he, most certainly, did not originate the recipe. A 1912 cookbook had two recipes for a "cream cheese pie" and one

for a "cream cheese cake"; one for small cheesecakes appeared in a 1909 issue of *The Boston Cooking-School Magazine*. Andrew Smith has suggested that New York bakeries and restaurants sold cheesecake made with Philadelphia Brand cream cheese, manufactured by Phenix, in the early 1900s. Cream cheese, however, does not appear to have found its way into the Jewish community during these times nor in the years that immediately followed. Not one of the Phenix ads in the *Forvertz* from 1920–27 suggests using Philadelphia Brand cream cheese in cheesecake. A 1922 recipe in the *Brooklyn Daily Eagle* suggests using two cups of cottage cheese pressed through a fine sieve (Anderson 390; M. and A. Batterberry 263; Breakstone Bros., "Cheesecake has a wonderful taste," 8 July 1925, see also, 8 May 1925; "Cheesecake"; Giendandt 15–16, 117; Marks, "American Cakes"; Marks, *Encyclopedia* 111; Joan Nathan, *Jewish Cooking in America* 184, 334; Smith, "Cheesecake" 103.)

27. For a detailed history of butter, see Visser (83–100).
28. The demise of *schmaltz* was also reflected in language. By 1937, *schmaltz* was already being employed, in English, as a derogatory term for "straight" jazz. It soon became a word applied to any artistic endeavor that had exaggerated sentimentalism (Diner, *Hungering* 212; Heinze 176–77; Joselit 187; Ruhlman; Steig; Webb 179; Wex 87–88, 91–93, 102–03).
29. A recent interview with Mark Russ Federman, the third-generation former-owner of Russ and Daughters appetizing store, said of his salt-cured lox: "His lox oozes with ocean, begging for cream cheese to counter the saltiness." Cream cheese is a good balance to lox because the triglycerides (complex fatty acids) in cream cheese not only soften and melt slowly in the mouth, creating the sensation of "creaminess," but they also, aided by proteins, coat the tongue, serving as a partial blocker to the salt receptors. Butter, lacking these proteins, disperses more quickly in the mouth, and so is not as effective as cream cheese in blocking salt (Brighenti ii, 66; Kinetz; Lucey interview; Marks, *Encyclopedia* 371; Schwartz, *Jewish Home Cooking* 159; "Raw Truth About Lox").
30. Though, following the stock market crash in 1929, food prices went down as did income (Sheffield Farms Stores; *Chicago Daily News Almanac* 711; "Retail Food Prices, 1925"). In a 1938 short story, one of the Jewish characters, attending a bridal shower, notes cream cheese and lox among the various dishes on the table and exclaims: "a regella blowout you got here!" Clearly, these were still expensive foods for some (Kober 25).
31. For a detailed look at the second generation of Eastern European Jewish immigrants, see Dash Moore.
32. For Oldenburg's work on "third places" see *Great Good Place*.
33. The entry of women into previously male realms and the increased co-mingling of the sexes had been steadily at work in downtown New York by at least 1910 as women increasingly became part of the work force, and Broadway cafes and

restaurants filled with "a hodge-podge" of young men and women. The 1920s saw the heyday of Horn & Hardart Automats where female clerks and typists sat side by side with male businessmen, and, following Prohibition, speakeasies became mixed as well. While Jewish daughters had been needed breadwinners for their immigrant families since the 1880s, and while socializing with the opposite sex was not novel—young Jewish women had, since that time, mingled together with men on the Lower East Side in sweatshops (sometimes uneasily), on the streets, in classrooms, cafes and dancehalls—nonetheless, the 1920s expanded their freedoms, rights (suffrage), and power (Batterberry 199, 206–07; Bender 110, 112–15; Glenn 79–85; Grimes 168–69, 180, 190–93, 205, 233; Kessner 88–91).

34. The entertainer, Al Jolson, for example, was known for inviting the whole audience (viz. men *and* women) to join him after the theatre at Lindy's. Merwin points out that the ("traditional") delicatessen had been a social setting for a particular Jew, the Jewish male, and calls attention to the sexual connotations of the *ongeshtupped* (overstuffed) sandwich. In a discrete footnote, he lists the sexual references attached to salamis and other deli meats. I would add that in a late 1920s Reuben's menu, the majority of the specialty sandwiches (meant to be held with two hands before being consumed), were named after women (Grimes 205, 207; Merwin, *Pastrami on Rye* 9, 60).
35. In 1927 alone, 264 new plays and musicals opened on Broadway (Bloom 299; Diner, *Hungering* 201–02; Grimes 205; Merwin, *Pastrami on Rye* 3, 6, 55–56, 62–63, 68). For a detailed treatment of Broadway during the "Roaring Twenties" and the gangster as a model conspicuous consumer, see Alexander; Charyn; and Ruth. For the involvement of Jews in vaudeville, Broadway shows, and film, and their position as heroes and role models for the second-generation immigrant Jewish community, see Merwin, *In Their Own Image*.
36. In December of 2016, strictly in the interests of scholarship, I visited Carnegie Deli of New York, just two weeks before its final closing, to investigate its "over-stuffed" corned beef sandwich. A careful weighing (before my liberal application of mustard) determined that it consisted of a pound (!) of meat between two slices of rye bread. Even though this amount, due to deli sandwich wars in the 1970s and 1980s, was probably larger than the over-stuffed sandwich of the late 1920s, nonetheless, the 1920s sandwich probably contained at least one-half pound of meat which, still, would have been quite a display. In his description of Lindy's deli (opened in 1921) Grimes called The Lindy's Special (turkey, tongue, Swiss cheese, coleslaw and Russian dressing) "a two-hander" ("An Obituary for the Carnegie Deli"; Grimes 205).
37. It should be noted that though cream cheese and Nova Scotia salmon are listed as separate items in a 1922 Reuben's menu, the cream cheese and lox combination does not appear there. The combination does turn up in the 1930s, albeit without the bagel, at Reuben's (The Ginger Rogers: salmon, cream cheese, and french-fried onions) and at Lindy's (Nova Scotia salmon and cream cheese) (Batterberry 263;

"Week of a New Yorker"; James; Levenstein 185–87; "Menu," Lindy's Delicatessen; "Menu," Reuben's Restaurant; Paddleford, "How Reuben's Lives Up"; Manoff; Marks, *Encyclopedia* 211; Merwin, *Pastrami on Rye* 7; *Mogen Dovid* 5; J. Nathan, *Jewish Cooking in America* 184, 334; "Reuben's"; "Sandwiches Flourishing").

38. Though a cream cheese and Bar le Duc (currant jelly) sandwich and a smoked whitefish with Russian dressing sandwich were among the fifty-seven varieties enumerated in the 1926 list, cream cheese and lox was not mentioned (G. J. Nathan 237–38).
39. This reason is, also, I would suspect, why chicken soup, though immediately identifiable as a Jewish food, did not achieve the iconic status of corned beef on rye or bagels and lox: neither the quantity nor the ingredients of chicken soup could convey the eater's upwardly mobile status (US Department of Labor 9–10, 36; Grimes 203–04; Kraut 411; Merwin, *In Their Own Image* 10 and *Pastrami on Rye* 7, 54–61; Mintz 98; Dash Moore 67; Heinze 8, 14–15; G. J. Nathan 237; Wilk, "Paradoxes of Jews" 238–42). For parallel examples of Italian "eating up," their adoption of American foods, and the iconic rise of macaroni, see Diner (*Hungering* 53–56). For the parallels between performance on Broadway and performance in Jewish assimilation and acculturation see Most.
40. This connection had to have occurred before the 1930s, since, following the stock market crash in October of 1929, theatre and nightclub life drastically declined, as did the excesses of the "Jazz Age" (Charyn 61, 223; Merwin, *In Their Own Image* 162–63).
41. The number of Broadway Jewish stars who came from impoverished immigrant backgrounds and who made the theatre district deli their "home" is legion: they include Irving Berlin, Walter Winchell, Al Jolson, Fanny Brice, the Marx Brothers and others. Contrast, as noted above, the thin, half ounce slice of lox per person consumed by immigrant families on the Lower East Side with today's bagel and lox combination that contains four to five and a half ounces of lox (ten times the amount!). Even, if—thanks to supersizing that begin in the 1980s—the amount of lox on a bagel in the 1920s was somewhat smaller than today, it still would have been many times the amount that most theater district deli customers had consumed in their youth. In 1930, for example, a "regular" smoked salmon sandwich (not overstuffed) consisted of three ounces of lox, six times the amount that second generation immigrants had eaten as children (Charyn 121–22; Grimes 205; Levine; "Fair Price List" 14).
42. Though Jolson appeared on the *Kraft Music Hall* (originally, *Kraft Musical Review*) broadcasts from 1933–34, it was only as a featured singer, not as host. Moreover, only the announcer talked about a specific Kraft product during the set commercial times. John Platt, Kraft's advertising manager, insisted, in a 1938 speech, that advertising and entertainment be kept separate on the show. Though the radio show

did have some commercials devoted to Philadelphia Brand cream cheese, given that Kraft was not pitching this show for a specifically Jewish market, and given that bagels did not even begin to enter the consciousness of the American mainstream population until the mid-1940s—*The New York Times* had to explain to its readership that bagels were, "small, hard Jewish rolls with holes in the center"—makes it exceedingly unlikely that these commercials would be suggesting cream cheese with bagels ("Bronx Cheers"; Bullington 909–12; Dunning 386; Kinetz; *Kraft Music Hall*, 2 Oct., 16 Oct., 23 Oct., 6 Nov., 27 Nov., 4 Dec., 18 Dec., 25 Dec. 1947; J. Nathan, *Jewish Cooking in America* 40; A. Schwartz 159).

43. Jolson never sang a song by this title. *Bagels and Yox* was a Broadway musical that opened in 1951, long after the combination of bagels, cream cheese, and lox had become popular in the Jewish community (Hischak 32; A. Schwartz 159).
44. I disagree, here, with both Berg's and Feinsilver's contention that the second-generation were all rejecting the food of their youth (Berg 255; Feinsilver, "Bagel Shmear" 11).
45. See, for example, "The Seasons," which noted that, "Friday, Saturday and Sunday is usually the busiest part of the week" without singling out Sunday brunch. See also "Bagale" and Paddleford, "Bagels and Lox." Murray Lender, of Lender's Bagels, recalled that by the mid-1950s, the majority of his bagels were sold on Sunday mornings, suggesting that it took some time for the Sunday morning ritual to become popular in the Jewish community (Diner, *Lower East Side* 63; Horowitz 205; J. Nathan, "Bagels" 32; Merwin, *Pastrami on Rye* 76, 88; J. Nathan, *Jewish Cooking in America* 83; Smith, "Brunch" 85; Ternikar 10–11, 57, 71).
46. I would suggest that the reasons for Sunday morning consumption should be sought in the rising economic status for second-generation immigrant Jews that made not working on Sunday morning possible. Note, here, the contrast between the immigrant parents sitting with their family around the tenement kitchen table on Sunday mornings to do piecework for the garment factories, with their second-generation children sitting around the Sunday morning table in the 1940s for brunch, "a meal of leisure, comfort, and often decadence in the American cultural imagination." Exceptions to New York's Blue Laws that allowed delicatessens to be opened on Sunday mornings no doubt played a role as well (Laband and Heinbuch 109–12; Kraut 413; Merwin, *Pastrami on Rye* 40–45; Batya Miller 269–86; Ternikar 29).
47. In what seems to be an unintentional parody of Levi-Straus' structural analysis, Regelson concludes that the transgression is even deeper than the violation of kosher rules; cream cheese and lox symbolize the negation of the incest taboo! (Regelson 136). Yet, in spite of this conclusion, and though his social setting date is not correct, his initial symbolic reading of the combination is a possible one. I argue, however, that this symbolic meaning was not in and of itself the causal factor for the creation of the bagels and lox combination but merely a possible contributing

one (Diner, *Hungering* 183–85, 205–06; Gabaccia 108; Glazer 60–61; Joselit 171–77, 214–16; Merwin, *Pastrami on Rye* 55, 79–80; Reuben's menu, circa 1929; Tuchman and Levine 169–70, 172–74).

48. Note also the quip that lox is "herring with high blood pressure" (Feinsilver, *Taste of Yiddish* 193).

Works Cited

"1920's Food and Groceries Prices." *The People History*, www.thepeoplehistory.com/20sfood.html. Accessed June 2016.

"Abraham Thompson." *1901 England Census, Ancestry.com*, www.ancestry.com. Digital image.

"Abram Thompson." *1891 England Census, Ancestry.com*, www.ancestry.com. Digital image.

Abusch-Magder, Ruth. "Eating 'Out': Food and the Boundaries of Jewish Community and Home in Germany and the United States." *Nashim: A Journal of Jewish Women's Studies and Gender Issues*, no. 5, 2002, pp. 53–82.

Alexander, Michael. *Jazz Age Jews*. Princeton Univ., 2001.

"An Alleged $40,000 Thief." *The Sun* [New York, NY], 26 March 1897.

Anderson, Jean. *The American Century Cookbook*. Clarkson Potter, 1997.

"An Obituary for the Carnegie Deli." *The Atlantic*, 1 Oct. 2016.

"The Appetizing Stores of New York." Jews of New York-Restaurants/Food, in Federal Writers' Project, Works Projects Administration, c. 1940. Unpublished manuscript.

"At H. Forman & Son, Salmon Smokers." *Spitalfields Life*, 4 Aug. 2011, www.spitalfieldslife.com/2011/08/04/at-h-forman-son-salmon-smokers/. Accessed April 2017.

"Bagale, Lox & Cream Cheese Service, Any Amount, Delivered at Your Door Each Sunday Morning Before Nine O'clock." *The Kingston Daily Freeman* [Kingston, NY], 29 May 1948, p. 9.

Balinska, Maria. *The Bagel: The Surprising History of a Modest Bread*. Yale Univ., 2008.

———. Letter to Josh Friedland, cited in "Jewish American Girl Doll Eats Bagels Sans Schmear," *The Food Section*, www.thefoodsection.com/foodsection/2009/07/jewish-american-girl-doll-eats-bagels-sans-schmear.html. Accessed 13 July 2009.

Batt, Alan. *The Great Bagel & Lox Book*. Battman Studios, 2004.

Batterberry, Michael and Ariane. *On the Town in New York: The Landmark History of Eating, Drinking, and Entertainments from the American Revolution to the Food Revolution*. Routledge, 1999.

Beitcher, Nick. Tartine Bakery, San Francisco. Personal Interview. May 2017.

Belasco, Warren. "Ethnic Fast Foods: The Corporate Melting Pot." *Food and Foodways*, vol. 2, 1987, pp. 1–29;

Bender, Daniel E. *Sweated Work, Weak Bodies: Anti-Sweatshop Campaigns and Languages of Labor*. Rutgers Univ., 2004.

Ben-Dov, Avigdor. Correspondence concerning the diet of his father, Beryl Root (b. 1891) in Zawady, Poland. 30 Oct. 2012.

Berg, Jennifer. "From the Big Bagel to the Big Roti? The Evolution of New York City's Jewish Food Icons." *Gastropolis: Food & New York City*, edited by Annie Hauck-Lawson and Jonathan Deutsch, Columbia Univ., 2009, pp. 252–73.

Berle, Milton. "My Mother's Boy." *The Sentinel* [Chicago], 8 April 1937.

Bittman, Mark. "Bagels, Lox and Me." *The New York Times*, 29 April 2014.

Bloom, Ken. *Broadway: Its History, People, and Places: An Encyclopedia*. Routledge, 2012.

Bobrow-Strain, Aaron. *White Bread: A Social History of the Store-Bought Loaf*. Beacon, 2012.

Braun, H. *Dos Familien Kokh-Bookh*. Hebrew, 1914. Edited and translated by Bracha B. Weingrod as *The Yiddish Family Cookbook*. Privately Published, 2010.

"Bread and Filth Cooked Together." *The Press* [New York], 30 Sept. 1894.

Breakstone Bros. "Cheesecake has a wonderful taste." *Forvertz*, 8 May 1925. Advertisement.

———. "Cheesecake has a wonderful taste." *Forvertz*, 8 July 1925. Advertisement.

———. "Cheese Kreplach." *Forvertz*, 17 June 1925. Advertisement.

———. "Downsville Cream Cheese." *Forvertz*, 6 Feb. 1924. Advertisement.

———. "Downsville Cream Cheese." *Forvertz*, 13 Feb. 1924. Advertisement.

———. "Downsville Cream Cheese." *Forvertz*, 2 June 1925. Advertisement.

———. "Downsville Cream Cheese." *Forvertz*, 17 June 1925. Advertisement.

———. "Downsville Cream Cheese." *Forvertz*, 5 Aug 1925. Advertisement.

———. "Downsville Cream Cheese." *Forvertz*, 16 March 1927. Advertisement.

———. "Give Your Children Bread Spread with Breakstone's Downsville Cream Cheese." *Forvertz*, 3 Dec. 1925. Advertisement.

———. "It Has a Fine Buttery Taste!" *Forvertz*, 20 Feb. 1924. Advertisement.

———. "Our Reputation is Your Protection." *Forvertz*, 15 April 1926. Advertisement.

———. "The Policeman." *Forvertz*, 25 Nov. 1925. Advertisement.

———. "Remember Our Label." *Forvertz*, 6 Feb. 1924. Advertisement.

———. "Tuviya the Dairyman Says." *Forvertz*, 8 May 1925. Advertisement.

Breakstone Bros. Cream cheese box, 5 lb., Breakstone Bros. Dairy Collection, National Museum of American Jewish History, Philadelphia, PA.

———. Cream cheese box, 5 lb., "Minimum Milk Fat Content 37%." Breakstone Bros. Dairy Collection.

———. "Cream Cheese with Lox" box, 2 lb., Breakstone Bros. Dairy Collection, c. 1927.

"Breakstone Bros." *Trow's New York City Directory*. The Trow City Directory Co., Trow's Printing and Bookbinding, 1897, 1898.

Breakstone Bros. Bronx Branch, Inc. "Certificate of Incorporation." 14 Nov. 1913, Break-stone file, Research Library, National Museum of American Jewish History, Philadelphia, PA.

Breakstone Bros., Inc., of New York, NY Breakstone's Downsville Brand. US Trademark 178,782, filed 22 May 1923, and issued 29 Jan. 1924.

Breakstone, Harry. Interview with Anita Solomon. November, 1966. Breakstone file, Research Library, National Museum of American Jewish History, Philadelphia, Pennsylvania.

Brenner, Paul. "The Formative Years of the Hebrew Bakers' Unions, 1881–1914." *YIVO Annual of Jewish Social Studies*, vol. 18, 1983, pp. 40–41.

Breskin, Nicole, Jenny Brown, and Jeff Otieno. "Rise of the Machines." *Losing Dough*, www.losingdough.com. Accessed Nov. 2016.

Brighenti, Mercedes. "Texture and Functionality of Cream Cheese." Dissertation, Univ. of Wisconsin-Madison, 2009.

"Bronx Cheers, Incognito, Protest New Bread Price." *The New York Times*, 31 May 1946.

Bullington, Michael R. "Kraft Foods, Inc." *The Advertising Age Encyclopedia of Advertising*, edited by John McDonough and Karen Egolf, Fitzroy Dearborn, 2003, pp. 909–12.

Charyn, Jerome. *Gangsters and Gold Diggers: Old New York, the Jazz Age, and the Birth of Broadway*. Thunder's Mouth, 2003.

"Cheesecake." *Brooklyn Daily Eagle*, 16 July 1922.

The Chicago Daily News Almanac and Year Book. Chicago Daily News, 1926.

Clift, W. "The Salmon and its Culture." *The Phrenological Journal and Science of Health*, vol. 55, no. 1, 1872, pp. 19–27.

Coates, Peter. *Salmon*. Reaktion, 2006.

Cohen, Lawrence A. *Anna's Shtetl*. Univ. of Alabama, 2007.

Cooper, John. *Eat and Be Satisfied: A Social History of Jewish Food*. Aronson, 1993.

Council of Jewish Women. *The Neighborhood Cookbook*. Portland: Bushong.

Dahlberg, Arthur C. "A New Method of Manufacturing Cream Cheese of the Neufchatel Type." *Journal of Dairy Science*, vol. 10, no. 2, 1927, pp. 106–16.

Danes-Wingett, Linda. "The Ice Car Cometh: A History of the Railroad Refrigerator Car." *The San Joaquin Historian*, vol. 10, no. 4, 1996, pp. 1–9.

Dash Moore, Deborah. *At Home in America: Second Generation New York Jews*. Columbia Univ., 1981.

"David Breakstone." *The New York Times*, 19 Sept. 1962.

Delaware Cheese Co. Inc. "Blue Bird Brand Cream Cheese." *Der Morgen Journal*, 16 Feb. 1920. Advertisement.

DeLoach, Barton. "Important Factors Affecting the Marketing of Canned Salmon." *American Marketing Journal*, vol. 2, no. 4, 1935, pp. 253–64.

Denker, Joel. *The World on a Plate: A Tour Through the History of America's Ethnic Cuisine*. Westview, 2003.

De Pomiane, Edourd. *Cuisine Juive Ghettos Moderne*. Michel, 1929.

Deutsch, Jonathan, and Rachel D. Saks. *Jewish American Food Culture*. Greenwood, 2008.

Diner, Hasia R. *Hungering for America: Italian, Irish, & Jewish Foodways in the Age of Migration*. Harvard Univ., 2001.

———. *Lower East Side Memories: A Jewish Place in America*. Princeton Univ., 2000.

Dion, Jill. "Local History: Milford's 'Bagel Beach' Was a Summer Haven for Jewish Families." *MilfordMirror.com*, 8 Aug. 2016, www.milfordmirror.com/tag/bagel-beach/. Accessed April 2017.

Ducat, Charles. Thompson Bagel Machine Mfg. Co. Personal Interview. October 2016.

Dunning, John. *On the Air: The Encyclopedia of Old Time Radio*. Oxford Univ., 1998.

Eisenstein, Judah David. *Otzar Zikhronotai*. Eisenstein, 1929.

Evans, Sara M. *Born for Liberty: A History of Women in America*. Free, 1989.

"The Fair Price List." *Mogen Dovid Delicatessen Magazine*, vol. 1, no. 1, 1930, p. 14.

Federman, Mark Russ. *Russ & Daughters: Reflections and Recipes From the House That Herring Built*. Schocken, 2013.

Feinsilver, Lilian Mermin. "The Bagel Shmear." *Present Tense*, vol. 3, 1975, pp. 9–12.

———. *The Taste of Yiddish*. 1970. Barnes, 1980.

Filipini, Alessandro. *The Table: How to Buy food, How to Cook it, and How to Serve It*. Baker & Taylor, 1895.

"Fire in Wallabout Market." *The Brooklyn Daily Eagle*, 12 March 1900.

Fishman, Sylvia Barack. *Jewish Life and American Culture*. State Univ. of New York, 2000.

Fox, Margalit. "Daniel Thompson, Whose Bagel Machine Altered the American Diet, Dies at 94." *The New York Times*, 21 Sept. 2015.

Freedman, Jonathan. *The Temple of Culture: Assimilation and Anti-Semitism in Literary Anglo-America*. Oxford Univ., 2000.

Freeman, Otis W. "Salmon Industry of the Pacific Coast." *Economic Geography*, vol. 11, no. 2, 1935, pp. 109–39.

Freeman, Beatrice and Ira Henry. "About: Bagels." *The New York Times*, 22 May 1960.

Gabaccia, Donna R. *We Are What We Eat: Ethnic Food and the Making of Americans*. Harvard Univ, 1998.

Gans, Herbert J. "Symbolic Ethnicity: The Future of Ethnic Groups and Cultures in America." *Ethnic and Racial Studies*, vol. 2, 1979, pp. 1–20.

Gantz, Carroll *Refrigeration: A History*. McFarland, 2015.

Gay, Ruth. *Unfinished People: Eastern European Jews Encounter America*. Norton, 1996.

Giendandt, Fritz. *The Twentieth Century Book for the Progressive Baker, Confectioner, Ornamenter, and Ice Cream Maker*. Privately Published, 1912.

Ginsberg, Stanley. *The Rye Baker: Classic Breads from Europe and America*. Norton, 2016.

Ginsberg, Stanley, and Norman Berg. *Inside the Jewish Bakery: Recipes and Memories from the Golden Age of Jewish Baking*. Camino Books, 2011.

Glass, Montague. "Kosher Restaurants." *Saturday Evening Post*, 3 Aug. 1929.

Glazer, Ruth. "The Jewish Delicatessen: The Evolution of an Institution." *Commentary*, vol. 1, 1945, pp. 58–63.

Glenn, Susan A. *Daughters of the Shtetl: Life and Labor in the Immigrant Generation*. Cornell Univ., 1990.

Goldstein, Eric L. *The Price of Whiteness: Jews, Race, and American Identity*. Princeton Univ., 2006.

Goodman, Matthew. "The Rise and Fall of the Bagel." *Harvard Review*, vol. 28, 2005, pp. 91–99.

Gosnell, Mariana. *Ice: The Nature, the History, and the Uses of an Astonishing Substance*. Univ. of Chicago, 2005.

Gostony, Adam. "Jews as Fish-consumers." Jews of New York-Restaurants/Food, Federal Writers' Project, Works Projects Administration, New York City Municipal Archives, New York, New York. Unpublished manuscript, 16 Feb. 1942.

Grader, Zeke. "A Brief History of Fish Processing in California and Oregon." *International Institute of Fisheries Economics & Trade 2000 Proceedings*, pp. 1–4, ir.library.oregonstate.edu/xmlui/bitstream/handle/1957/30929/167.pdf?sequence=1. Accessed Nov. 2016.

"Green Vegetables Short for Next Few Weeks." *Decatur Review*, 8 Feb. 1924.

Greenbaum, Florence Kreisler. *The International Jewish Cookbook*. Bloch, 1919.

Grimes, William. *Appetite City: A Culinary History of New York*. North Point, 2009.

Halter, Marilyn. *Shopping for Identity: The Marketing of Ethnicity*. Schocken, 2000.

Heinze, Andrew. *Adapting to Abundance: Jewish Immigration, Mass Consumption, and the Search for American Identity*. Columbia Univ., 1990.

Hine, Thomas. *The Total Package: The Secret History and Hidden Meanings of Boxes, Bottles, Cans, and Other Persuasive Containers*. Little, Brown, 1995.

Hischak, Thomas S. *Broadway Plays and Musicals*. McFarland, 2009.

Horowitz, Andy. "The Lender Family of New Haven, Connecticut." *The Jews in New Ha-ven*, Vol. IX, edited by David S. Fischer, Jewish Historical Society of Greater New Haven, 2009, p. 205.

Howard, Willie (William Levkowitz). "Tyrone Shapiro (The Bronx caballero)." Gala, undated. Eric Byron Collection, #1001-A, Ellis Island Discography Project, Museum Division of the Ellis Island Immigration Museum. 78 rpm.

Jacob, Heinrich Eduard. *Six Thousand Years of Bread: Its Holy and Unholy History*. 1944. Lyons, 1997.

James, Rian. "The Inky Way." *Brooklyn Daily Eagle*, 10 March 1929.

Jensen, William Sherman. "A Market Structure Analysis of the Salmon Processing In-dustry." Dissertation, Oregon State Univ., June, 1975.

Jewish Baker's Voice, 13 December 1929 in Balinska, *The Bagel*, 124.

Joselit, Jenna Weisman. *The Wonders of America: Reinventing Jewish Culture, 1880–1950*. Hill and Wang, 1994.

Kessner, Thomas. *The Golden Door: Italian and Jewish Immigrant Mobility in New York City 1880–1915*. Oxford Univ., 1977.

Kinetz, Erica. "So Pink, so New York." *The New York Times*, 22 Sept. 2002.

Kirshenblatt-Gimblett, Barbara. "Food and Drink." *YIVO Encyclopedia of Jews in Eastern Europe*, www.yivoencyclopedia.org/article.aspx/Food_and_Drink. Accessed June 2016.

Kisseloff, Jeff. *You Must Remember This: An Oral History of Manhattan from the 1890s to World War II*. Harcourt Brace Jovanovich, 1989.

Kober, Arthur. "Shower in the Bronx." *The New Yorker*, 7 May 1938, pp. 24–26.

Knight, Thomas F. *Shore and Deep Sea Fisheries of Nova Scotia*. Grant, 1867.

Kraft Music Hall. Old Time Radio Catalog, 2 Oct., 16 Oct., 23 Oct., 6 Nov. 6, 27 Nov., 4 Dec., 18 Dec., 25 Dec., 1947, www.otrcat.com/p/al-jolson. Accessed Feb. 2016.

Kraut, Alan M. "Ethnic Foodways: The Significance of Food in the Designation of Cultural Boundaries Between Immigrant Groups in the U.S., 1840–1921." *Journal of American Culture*, vol. 2, no. 3, 1979, pp. 409–420.

Laband, David N., and Deborah Hendry Heinbuch. *Blue Laws: The History, Economics, and Politics of Sunday-Closing Laws.* Heath, 1987.

Lederhendler, Eli. *Jewish Responses to Modernity: New Voices in America and Eastern Europe.* New York Univ., 1994.

Lem, Ellyn. "You Say 'Canape', and I Say 'Kreplach': Reading the Cultural Culinary Conflicts in Jewish American Writers." *Days of Wonder: Nights of Light*, special issue of *Studies in American Jewish Literature*, vol. 21, 2002, pp. 94–107.

Levenstein, Harvey A. *Revolution at the Table: The Transformation of the American Diet.* Oxford Univ., 1988.

Levine, Ed. "Was Life Better When Bagels Were Smaller?" *The New York Times*, 31 Dec. 2003.

Lewando, Fania. *Vegetarish-Dietisher Kokhbukh: 400 Shpeizn Gemakht Oysshlislekh fun Grinsn.* Vilna, 1938. Translated by Eve Jochnowitz as *The Vilna Vegetarian Cookbook.* Schocken, 2015.

Louis Kadans. "Yankee Cream Cheese." *Der Morgen Journal,* 19 Nov. 1918. Advertisement.

———. "Yankee Cream Cheese." *Der Morgen Journal*, 1 Dec. 1918. Advertisement.

———. "Yankee Cream Cheese: A Taste of Eden!" *Forvertz*, 17 April 1919. Advertisement.

"Lox and Bagel Country." *Lowell Sun*, 9 Dec. 1948.

Luce, Caroline. "Radicalism in the Ethnic Market—The Jewish Bakers Union of Los Angeles in the 1920s." Institute for Research on Labor and Employment, June 2010, www.escholarship.org/uc/item/53b6q84v. Accessed April 2017.

Lucey, John A. Department of Food Science, Univ. of Wisconsin-Madison. Personal Interview. April 2017.

Lundstedt, Erik. "Manufacture of Quality Cream Cheese." *Journal of Dairy Science*, vol. 37, no. 2, 1954, pp. 243–45.

Manoff, Arnold. "Reuben and His Restaurant: The Lore of a Sandwich." 18 Dec. 1938, American Life Histories: Manuscripts from the Federal Writers' Project, 1936–40, Manuscript Division, Library of Congress, www.loc.gov/item/wpalh001447/. Accessed Jan. 2016.

Marks, Gil. "American Cakes-New York Cheesecake." *Tori Avey*, www.toriavey.com/toris-kitchen/2014/07/new-york-cheesecake-history-recipe/. Accessed June 2016.

———. *Encyclopedia of Jewish Food.* Wiley, 2010.

Marx, Jeffrey A. "The Days Had Come of Curds and Cream: The Origins and Development of Cream Cheese in America, 1870–1880." *Food, Culture & Society*, vol. 15, no. 2, 2012, pp. 177–95.

———. "Philadelphia® Comes to New York: The Marketing of Cream Cheese in New York State." *New York History, Quarterly Journal of the New York State Historical Association and The State University of New York College at Oneonta*, vol. 96, no. 2, 2015, 184–96.

McCann, Alfred. "The Cheese of the Ancients and a Fine Modern Product." *Bronx Home News*, 11 July 1924.

"Menu." Reuben's Restaurant, 23 April 1922, The Henry Voigt Collection of American Menus, Henry Voigt, Wilmington, Delaware.

"Menu." Lindy's Delicatessen, c. 1935, The Henry Voigt Collection of American Menus, Henry Voigt, Wilmington, Delaware.

"Menu." Reuben's Restaurant.

Merwin, Ted. *In Their Own Image: New York Jews in Jazz Age Popular Culture*. Rutgers Univ., 1968.

———. *Pastrami on Rye: An Overstuffed History of the Jewish Deli*. New York Univ., 2015.

"Meyer Thompson." *U. S. Border Crossings from Canada to the U. S. 1895–1956*, www.ancestry.com. Digital image.

"Meyer Thompson." *U. S. Naturalization Record Indexes, 1791–1992*, www.ancestry.com. Digital image.

"Meyer Thompson." *U. S., Social Security Death Index, 19352014*, www.ancestry.com. Digital image.

Miller, Batya. "Enforcement of the Sunday Closing Laws on the Lower East Side, 1882–1903." *American Jewish History*, vol. 91, no. 2, 2003, 269–86.

Miller, Cyrus C. *Report of the Mayor's Market Commission of New York City*. Little & Ives, 1913.

Mink, Nicolaas. *Salmon: A Global History*. Reaktion, 2013.

Mintz, Sidney W. *Tasting Food, Tasting Freedom*. Beacon, 1996.

Mishnah Pesachim 10:4. *Mishnayoth*. Translated by Philip Blackman, Judaica, 1990.

Modan, Gabriella. "White, Whole Wheat, Rye: Jews and Ethnic Categorization in Washington, D.C." *Journal of Linguistic Anthropology*, vol. 11, no. 1, 2001, pp. 116–30.

Mogen Dovid Delicatessen Magazine, vol. 2, no. 4, 1932, p. 5.

Moss, Richard. "Racial Anxiety on the Comics Page: Harry Hershfield's 'Abie the Agent', 1914–1940." *The Journal of Popular Culture*, vol. 40, no. 1, 2007, pp. 90–108.

Most, Andrea. *Making Americans: Jews and the Broadway Musical*. Harvard Univ., 2004.

Nathan, George Jean. "Clinical Notes." *The American Mercury*, vol. 8, 1926, pp. 235–38.

Joan Nathan, "Bagels." *The Oxford Companion to American Food and Drink*, edited by Andrew F. Smith, Oxford Univ., 2007, p. 32.

———. *Jewish Cooking in America*. Knopf, 1994.

National Center for Jewish Film. "Horodok–Joseph Shapiro–home movies." 14:37:20. Steven Spielberg Film and Video Archive, United States Holocaust Memorial Museum.

Navarra, Tova. *The New Jersey Shore: A Vanishing Splendor*. Art Alliance, 1985.

Netboy, Anthony. *The Atlantic Salmon: A Vanishing Species?* Houghton Mifflin, 1968.

———. *The Columbia River Salmon and Steelhead Trout: Their Fight for Survival*. Univ. of Washington, 1981.

"New Incorporations." *The New York Times*, 23 Nov. 1913.

O'Bannon, Patrick W. "Waves of Change: Mechanization in the Pacific Coast Canned-Salmon Industry, 1864–1914." *Technology and Culture*, vol. 28, no. 3, 1987, pp. 558–77.
"Of Interest to Women." *Brooklyn Daily Eagle*, 24 Dec. 1893.
Oldenburg, Roy. *The Great Good Place: Cafes, Coffee Shops, Bookstores, Bars, Hair Salons, and Other Hangouts at the Heart of a Community.* Marlowe, 1991.
O'Neill, Molly. "Bagels Are Now Fast Food, and Purists Do a Slow Boil." *The New York Times*, 25 April 1993.
Paddleford, Clementine. "Bagels and Lox Delivered for Breakfast in Bed." *New York Herald Tribune*, 5 Dec. 1947.
———. "How Reuben's Lives Up to Sandwich King Title." *Herald Tribune* [New York], 28 Dec. 1949.
Pasklinksi, Moyshe. "Shmuel Chaim der Rofe." *Sefer Kalushin*, Kalushiner Societies in Israel, the United States of America, Argentine, France and Other Countries, 1961, pp. 255–63.
"Pat Haba Bikisnin." *Halachipedia*, www.halachipedia.com/index.php?title=Pat_Haba_Bikisnin. Accessed Nov. 2016.
"People of a Thousand Towns: Online Photographic Catalogue." *YIVO Institute for Jewish Research*, yivo1000towns.cjh.org/search.asp. Accessed Oct. 2016,
Phenix. "Always Fresh, Always Good." *Forvertz*, 22 May 1920. Advertisement.
———. "Philadelphia Cream Cheese." *Forvertz*, 7 April 1920. Advertisement.
———. "Philadelphia Cream Cheese." *Forvertz*, 23 July 1920. Advertisement.
———. "Philadelphia Cream Cheese." *Forvertz*, 17 Aug. 1921. Advertisement.
———. "Philadelphia Cream Cheese." *Forvertz*, 15 Nov. 1922. Advertisement.
———. "Philadelphia Cream Cheese Hawaiian Salad." *The Evening World* [New York], 10 March 1920. Advertisement.
Philologos. "Now Shmear This." *Forvertz (Jewish Daily Forward)*, 10 Feb. 2006.
Publow, Charles A. *Fancy Cheeses for the Farm and Factory*, Bulletin 270. Agricultural Experiment Station of the College of Agriculture, Cornell Univ., 1909.
"The Raw Truth About Lox." *Forvertz* (Jewish Daily Forward), 11 July 2003.
Reese, Jonathan. *Refrigeration Nation: A History of Ice, Appliances, and Enterprise in America.* Johns Hopkins Univ., 2013.
Regelson, Stanley. "The Bagel: Symbol and Ritual at the Breakfast Table." *The American Dimension: Cultural Myths and Social Realities*, edited by W. Arens and Susan P. Montague, Alfred, 1976, pp. 124–38.
"Retail Food Prices, 1925." *Historical Text Archive*, www.historicaltextarchive.com/sections.php?action=read&artid=418. Accessed Nov. 2016.
"Reuben's." *New York Morning Telegraph*, 24 Jan. 1928.
Reuben's menu, circa 1929. "Roast Pork," "Home Boiled Ham." *Appetite City: A Culinary History of New York*, edited by William Grimes, North Point, 2009, p. 207.
R. L. Polk & Co. *Trow's New York City Street and Avenue Directory, Borough of Manhattan.* R. L. Polk & Co., 1915.

Roden, Claudia. *The Book of Jewish Food.* Penguin, 1999.

Rosenbaum, Mark S. "The Symbolic Servicescape: Your Kind Is Welcomed Here." *Journal of Consumer Behavior*, vol. 4, no. 4, 2005, pp. 257–67.

Roth, Geneen. *The Craggy Hole in My Heart and the Cat Who Fixed It: Over the Edge and Back with my Cat, My Dad, and Me.* Three Rivers, 2004.

Ruhlman, Michael. *The Book of Schmaltz: Love Song to a Forgotten Fat.* Little, Brown, 2013.

Ruth, David E. *Inventing the Public Enemy: The Gangster in American Culture, 1918–1934.* Univ. of Chicago, 1996.

"Sacramento Salmon Fisheries." *Christian Advocate and Journal*, vol. 28, no. 25, 1853, p. 100.

Sadow, Jonathan. "Bagels and Genres." *Voices*, vol. 37, 2011, pp. 3–9.

"Sandwiches Flourishing." *The New York Times*, 2 Nov. 1924.

Schneerson, Rabbi Menachem. Talk, 19 April 1986, www.chabad.org/library/article_cdo/aid/2511773/jewish/Shabbos-Parshas-Metzora-Shabbos-HaGadol-10th-Day-of-Nissan-5746-1986.htm. Accessed Oct. 2016.

Schwartz, Arthur. *Arthur Schwartz's Jewish Home Cooking.* Ten Speed, 2008.

Schwartz, Oded. *In Search of Plenty: A History of Jewish Food.* Culture Concepts, 1992.

"The Seasons." *Mogen Dovid Delicatessen Magazine*, vol. 2, no. 7, 1932, p. 13.

Sheffield Farms Stores. "Breakstone's Cream Cheese Lb. 49¢." *Brooklyn Daily Eagle*, 15 Jan. 1925. Advertisement.

Sheraton, Mimi. *The Bialy Eaters: The Story of a Bread and a Lost World.* Broadway, 2000.

———. "Lost, Then Found: New York Classics." *The New York Times*, 31 July 2012.

Slifkin, Natan. "The Evolution of the Olive: The Halachic History of the Expanding Kezayis." *Rationalist Judaism*, 2014, www.RationalistJudaism.com, pp. 1–28. Accessed November, 2016.

Smith, Andrew F. "Brunch." *Savoring Gotham: A Food Lover's Companion to New York City*, edited by Andrew F. Smith, Oxford Univ., 2015, p. 85.

———. "Cheesecake." *Savoring Gotham: A Food Lover's Companion to New York City*, edited by Andrew F. Smith, Oxford Univ., 2015, p. 103.

———. *New York City: A Food Biography.* Rowman and Littlefield, 2013.

Solnit, Rebecca. "Winged Mercury and the Golden Calf." 2006. *The Encyclopedia of Trouble and Spaciousness*, edited by Rebecca Solnit, Trinity Univ., 2014, pp. 95–108.

Stacy's Bagel Chips. *Stacy's*, www.stacyssnacks.com. Accessed May 2017.

Stampfer, Shaul. "Bagel and Falafel: Two Iconic Jewish Foods and One Modern Jewish Identity." *Jews and Their Foodways,* edited by Anat Heiman, Oxford Univ., 2015, pp. 187–89.

State of New York Dept. of Agriculture. *Butter and Cheese Factories, Milk Stations and Condenseries in the State of New York, 1906,* Bulletin No. 8, 1907, p. 93.

Steig, Henry Anton. "Profiles: Alligators' Idol." *The New Yorker*, 17 April 1937.

Tene, Ofra. "'The New Immigrant Must Not Only Learn, He Must Also Forget': The Making of Eretz Israeli Ashkenazi Cuisine." *Jews and Their Foodways*, edited by Anat Heiman, Oxford Univ., 2015, pp. 46–64.

Ternikar, Farha. *Brunch: A History.* Rowman & Littlefield, 2014.

"Things You Never Hear." *Mogen Dovid Delicatessen Magazine*, vol. 8, no. 1, 1937, p. 10.

Thompson, Daniel T. "History and Development of the Bagel Machine." *Thompson Bagel Machine*, 2013, www.bagelproducts.com/bagel_formers/history.htm. Accessed August 2016.

Trillin, Calvin. "The Magic Bagel." *The New Yorker*, 27 March 2000, pp. 53–58, 87–89.

The Trow City Directory Co., 1899.

The Trow City Directory Co., 1900.

The Trow City Directory Co., 1902.

Tuchman, Gaye, and Harry Gene Levine. "New York Jews and Chinese Food: The Social Construction of an Ethnic Pattern." *The Taste of American Place: A Reader on Regional and Ethnic Foods*, edited by Barbara G. Shortridge and James R. Shortridge, Rowman & Littlefield, 1998, pp. 163–84.

"Tyrone Shapiro." *Billboard*, 21 August 1943, p. 67.

US Department of Labor. *Bulletin of the U. S. Bureau of Labor Statistics*, No. 445, 1927.

United States Tariff Commission. *Tariff Information Surveys on Articles in Paragraphs 717 and 718 of the Tariff Act of 1922: Salmon*. US Government Printing Office, 1929.

Visser, Margaret. *Since Eve Ate Apples: Much Depends on Dinner.* Grove, 1986.

Wasserman, Suzanne. "Hawkers and Gawkers: Peddling and Markets in New York City." *Gastropolis: Food & New York City*, edited by Annie Hauck-Lawson and Jonathan Deutsch, Columbia Univ., 2009, pp. 153–73.

Webb, H. Brook. "The Slang of Jazz." *American Speech*, vol. 12, no. 3, 1937, pp. 179–84.

Weber, Donald. *Haunted in the New World: Jewish American Culture from Cahan to the Goldbergs*. Indiana Univ., 2005.

"The Week of a New Yorker." *Brooklyn Daily Eagle*, 18 Feb. 1929.

Wex, Michael. *Rhapsody in Schmaltz: Yiddish Food and Why We Can't Stop Eating It.* St. Martin's, 2016.

Wilk, Richard. *Home Cooking in the Global Village: Caribbean Food from Buccaneers to Ecotourists.* Berg, 2006.

Wilk, Richard. "Paradoxes of Jews and Their Foods." *Jews and Their Foodways,* edited by Anat Heiman, Oxford Univ., 2015, pp. 231–48.

Yezierska, Anzia. *Hungry Hearts.* 1920. Penguin, 1997.

Young, Daniel. "The Bagel's New York Accent is Fading." *The New York Times*, 6 Sept. 1989.

Zanger, Mark. "Ethnic Food." *The Oxford Companion to American Food and Drink*, edited by Andrew F. Smith, Oxford Univ., 2007, pp. 208–10.

Zara, Louis. *Blessed is the Man.* Bobbs-Merrill, 1935.

Zborowski, Mark, and Elizabeth Herzog. *Life Is With People: The Culture of the Shtetl.* Schocken, 1952.

The Feast at the End of the Fast: The Evolution of an American Jewish Ritual*

by Nora L. Rubel

There is a famous scene in Woody Allen's 1977 film *Annie Hall*, where the Jewish protagonist Alvie Singer visits his girlfriend's family for Easter Dinner. In a split screen imagined exchange between Annie's mother and Allen's family at their respective dinner tables, the matriarch asks how the Jewish family will be spending "the holidays." Mrs. Singer immediately replies, "We fast." Mr. Singer chimes in, "Yeah, no food. You know, we have to atone for our sins." Mrs. Hall responds, "What sins? I don't understand." And Mr. Singer, still shoveling food in his mouth replies, "Tell you the truth, neither do we."

Most attention to Jewish foodways involves examining the act of eating rather than that of not eating. Whether it be the ritualized foods of the Passover Seder or the conspicuous consumption at life-cycle celebrations such as bar and bat mitzvahs and weddings, scholars of foodways have an embarrassment of riches handed to them on a quasi-kosher plate. As Jenna Weissman Joselit has observed in her work on American Jews in the mid- twentieth century, "In lieu of going to *shul* or attending temple, the overwhelming majority of American Jews honed their sense of ritual not in the sanctuary but in the dining room, where they believed . . . that 'the array of traditional foods . . . is the flour that nourishes Judaism'" (*Wonders of America* 219). But the Jewish ritual year calls for abstention from food on at least six occasions, the most well known and observed fast being that of the Day of Atonement, Yom Kippur. According to the 2000–01 National Jewish Population Survey, 60 percent of American Jews fast on Yom Kippur, a number that is significantly higher than the percentage belonging to synagogues (47 percent) (United Jewish Communities). The percentage of fasters rises to 79 percent if one looks only at those synagogue-affiliated Jews; this percentage comes close to the 83 percent who light Chanukah candles and dwarfs the weekly lighting of Shabbat candles (48 percent). This practice of fasting is most common in communities with large Jewish populations, amusingly noted by a city study in the 1980s which concluded that "the non-Jewish spouse of a Jew in Baltimore was more likely to fast on Yom Kippur than a born Jew in San Francisco" (Fishman 129).

But this essay is not about *not* eating. In many religious cultures, feasting follows a fast. The traditional Catholic fast days of Christmas Eve and the Lenten season's Ash Wednesday are followed by the feasts of Christmas Day and Easter. The month-long daily fasts of Ramadan are followed by joyous *iftars* after sundown. It is, in fact, surprising that the twenty-five hour fast of Yom Kippur would *not* be directly followed by an elaborate feast. But traditionally—for a variety of economic and cultural factors—immediate post-fast feasting has not been the practice of Ashkenazi (Eastern European) Jews. Feasting did traditionally occur in the form of delayed gratification during the holiday of Sukkot, four days later. However, no longer content to anticlimactically sip a sweet glass of tea and nosh on a dry piece of honey cake left over from Rosh Hashanah, American Jews invented a break fast of their own.

In *We Are What We Celebrate*, Amitai Etzioni refers to both lightly edited and wholly engineered holidays, remarking that such "modifications . . . both reflect changes in values and power relations and help to formulate and ensconce changes in values and power" (30). The creation of the new American break fast likewise reflects the changing values and priorities of contemporary Jewish American culture alongside changes in American Jewish identity and practice. This essay will address the historical and cultural evolution of the break fast among American Jews in the latter decades of the twentieth century as well as explore its significance as an indicator of changing views of religious authority.

THE HIGHEST OF THE HIGH HOLY DAYS

As Orthodox rabbi Irving Greenberg has noted:

> Many American Jews who have allowed their observance of tradition to diminish still observe Yom Kippur. This is a day of deprivation and denial, of guilt and self-flagellation. If Yom Kippur is their only

> contact with Judaism, one can only say: "O Lord, who is like your people, Israel?" What kind of devotion keeps people coming back year after year to a service that is long, exhausting, and solemn? (118)

The majority of American Jews do not attend religious services more than a few times a year, so why do so many continue to fast on Yom Kippur (Pew Forum)? This question is not new among spectators of American Jewish life. In a 1959 study of suburban Jews, Albert Gordon suggested several motives for this observance: "Nostalgia; the feeling that parents, near or far, would approve; the conventions of society . . . ; [and] the urging of one's children." Almost as an afterthought he writes, "There are those, too, who worship and pray in all sincerity and truth to a God in Whom they believe without equivocation or uncertainty" (136). It does seem however, at least to Gordon, that these latter Jews are a distinct minority and it is clear that the infrequent worship patterns of American Jews are not a recent occurrence.

In their 1967 study on Jewish identity and practice, sociologists Marshall Sklare and Joseph Greenblum examined the reasons why some rituals were retained by American Jews and why others were abandoned. Their findings determined that rituals were most likely to be retained when the ritual is, among other things: "capable of effective redefinition in modern terms, does not demand social isolation or the adoption of a unique lifestyle, [and] accords with the religious culture of the larger community and provides a 'Jewish' alternative which is felt to be needed" (50–55). Selective observance is nothing new, particularly when the rituals that are retained can be imbued with contemporary meaning.[1] This fast can be broken down according to Sklare and Greenblum's findings. First, fasting on Yom Kippur can be redefined as a physical purification akin to a contemporary "cleanse" detoxification diet or can be seen as spiritually purifying on a variety of other levels. While many people fast as a repentant effort to have God hear their prayers, others may take advantage of this day's hunger pains to think of those who have no food.[2] Second, fasting on Yom Kippur—unlike adopting a strictly kosher lifestyle—is a twenty-five hour annual experiment; once over, there is no need to look back. And finally, and possibly most powerfully, other Jews are doing it all over the world at the same time. Fasters may feel linked to their ancestors and their community through this annual shared experience. As Martha Finch notes in her work on Puritan feasts and fasts, "suffering with others the discomforts of food deprivation . . . produced intense feelings of social bonding" (38). Likewise, the cessation of fasting with others in a shared celebration of bounty is also a bonding ritual.

BREAKING THE FAST

Historically, scant attention has been paid to the cuisine or etiquette surrounding the meal following the Yom Kippur fast in America. We can turn for evidence of this omission to Jewish cookbooks. As Barbara Kirschenblatt-Gimblett has noted, "Cookbooks, though not direct indications of what people ate, nevertheless represent Jewish cuisine and social life," and twentieth century cookbooks, with a few noted exceptions, do not make mention of this meal with any detail until the last decades of the century (77). The 1954 *Jewish Festival Cookbook* explains the evening following fasting thus: "All now return home to a meal as simple or elaborate as the family desires, and they while away the time before dinner is ready drinking coffee and nibbling on apples dipped in honey, and on *honey lekach* or coffee cake" (Engle and Blair 54). The authors offer a "Dinner to Break the Fast" menu, but it is a soup-to-nuts meal that includes "Chicken Soup" and "Roast Duck or Chicken," certainly not a ready-made buffet in waiting. A 1957 Ohio congregational cookbook merely comments that on "Yom Kippur night sweet and sour fish or herring is used to break the fast" (Anshe Chesed Congregation and Rousuck 7). Jennie Grossinger's *The Art of Jewish Cooking,* a standard midcentury Jewish cookbook, gives absolutely no mention of this meal and her book's foreword briefly describes the meal that precedes the fast, only to suggest that it be hearty but relatively bland—in order "to prevent undue thirst" (xii). Under "Suggested Menus for the Principal Holidays," Yom Kippur does not appear. This is representative of most American Jewish cookbooks up to this point.

Elaborating a bit on the domestic practice of this festival, the popular 1964 *Guide for the Jewish Homemaker* suggests, "At home a light meal is eaten, a 'break the fast' meal." Under "Basic Holy Days Menus" the authors write: "To Break the Fast (Often this is a very light meal, almost like a breakfast): (*Suggestion*) Orange Juice, Eggs, Cheeses, Cold Fish, Salad, Cake, Coffee" (Levi and Kaplan 90). While these few cookbooks make brief mention of the ritual of breaking the fast, they offer no recipes and certainly don't indicate a large gathering. More common in the late sixties was the appearance of extensive menus for the prefast dinner, complete with information on how to most healthily prepare for the fast. The 1972 *A Taste of Tradition* offers such a menu for the pre-fast dinner and remarks briefly on the break fast: "Now, light refreshments are taken; perhaps a cup of tea and a delicate sweet. A little later, dinner that suits the personal preferences of each family is enjoyed. Some like salty foods, such as herring, to compensate for the loss of body salts; others prefer dairy dishes" (Sirkis 17). Again, this does not suggest more than some familial snacking to soothe the day's hunger pains.

While midcentury advice like the above describes a light family supper, later evidence from the 1980s and 1990s suggests a modern tradition of feasting, more reminiscent of those the high priests enjoyed after the Yom Kippur sacrifices at the Temple, a meal that is not "complete without a towering display of bagels, heaps of whitefish salad, ample platters of smoked salmon—and a houseful of hungry guests" (Joselit, "Breaking Down"). The 1990s and first decade of the 2000s have seen magazines, cookbooks, and even supermarkets (with their enticing catering menus) give rise to new ideas regarding this feast—generally referred to as the break fast. The Internet, with blogs available on all elements of religious practice—as well as dietary interests—is no exception. Conservative practitioners still tend to urge a tradition of moderation in breaking the fast, but contemporary publications frequently suggest a more satisfying—and filling—gastronomical conclusion to the day's supplications.

In the 1999 *Jewish Holiday Style*, the authors write: "This buffet is fun. Everyone is feeling wonderful, and everyone is starved, the perfect combination for a successful meal. At the conclusion of Yom Kippur, the havdalah prayer is recited over a cup of wine, and a festive meal is served" (Brownstein and Koplowitz 24).[3] They claim that it is customary to invite people over and offer an extensive menu with large numbers of servings per recipe. In 2008's *Jewish Holiday Cooking*, the author offers a story about break fasts before providing menus and recipes. She writes of a friend dying of pancreatic cancer who threw a break fast in her last year:

> Phyllis had not intended her guest list to be Jewish, but this being Manhattan, as it turned out everyone who wasn't Jewish had a Jewish connection: a spouse or a parent, a loved one who was. And though only some of us had fasted, the delicious festive meal—catered smoked fish and salads from Russ and Daughters on the Lower East Side and home-baked desserts—tasted sacred to us all. (Cohen 186)

Of course, through the contemporary availability of Jewish cookbooks that highlight the exotic cultures of Jews outside of Eastern Europe, one is no longer restricted to the traditional blintzes and bagels of Ashkenazi cuisine (Goldstein, *Sephardic Flavors*; Goldstein, *Saffron Shores*). One could break her fast with almond milk as the Iraqi or Indian Jews do, or with a spiced anise bread as Algerian Jews do, or with the delicious hearty bean soup known as *harira* that the Moroccan Jews adopted from their Ramadan-observant Muslim neighbors.[4] The popular culinary Website Epicurious.com has even offered a "Mix-and-match Yom Kippur menu-maker for the Break Fast" ("Break the Fast"). The menu suggestions found in these contemporary cookbooks, magazines and Websites for this meal again reflect the shift from a traditionally modest break fast to a far more lavish brunch-style event. Despite what appears to be a rather high-class problem of deciding what to serve, the significance of participation in this new ritual should not be underappreciated.

Cookbooks are not the only evidence of the growing popularity of this ritualized gathering. A 2003 essay in the Jewish weekly *Forward* found an author declaring:

> [W]hen a dish is not only delicious but also happens to be among those traditionally eaten at the close of Yom Kippur—when you join yourself with other Jews not just in the fasting, but in the eating as well—it becomes greater still, by satisfying more than one kind of hunger. (Food Maven)

What are these foods that are "traditionally eaten"? The assumption is that it is "Jewish" food—a subject too broad for the scope of this paper, as this category can include both bagels and lo mein.[5] Given a survey of Jewish cookbooks—both commercial and communal—that describe this meal, the most popular foods are dairy foods that can be served cold, essentially a brunch-style meal.[6] This eating of agreed-upon Jewish food at the close of Yom Kippur reflects what Herbert Gans described in his 1979 essay on "symbolic ethnicity" which he defined as "a nostalgic allegiance . . . a love for and pride in a tradition that can be felt without having to be incorporated in everyday behavior" (9). However, the *Forward* writer suggests that by eating foods one identifies as Jewish, and by eating with other Jews, this ritualized Jewish experience can be more than just symbolic; it can be transformative.

In an essay in the Jewish journal, *ZEEK*, Marilyn Sneiderman, executive director of AVODAH: The Jewish Service Corps, describes her annual break fast practice:

> Every year, . . . my family hosts a Yom Kippur Breakfast for 200 or so of our Jewish and non-Jewish friends. It is a time we reflect on what is going on in the world, ask ourselves what role we've played in challenging injustice, and recommit ourselves as a group to work for justice. I will never forget when we gathered after 9/11. Three of us led prayers, mine in Hebrew, a Christian friend in English, and a Muslim friend in Arabic. At a moment of such despair, it was incredibly

> powerful for our community, made up of people of different races and faiths, to join together on Yom Kippur to rededicate ourselves to rising above hate.

Unlike Jewish holidays like Passover, Chanukah, or even Tu B'Shvat, which can be celebrated for their universalist themes and home-based practice, Yom Kippur is a different holiday entirely—one that speaks specifically to the relationship between Jews and their God, and takes place primarily in the synagogue. But in the way that Sneiderman has crafted her break fast, she has been able to redefine Yom Kippur as potentially universal—a holiday that can be shared with non-Jews. Notably, she also redefines her community.

The solemnity of Yom Kippur traditionally is set apart from the more familiar food-centered Jewish calendar year, but with this increased popularity of the break fast party, the holiday becomes a bit more palatable to those Jews who enjoy the time with family and friends but may be less likely to spend the day in organized prayer. Cookbook author Joan Nathan, in her comprehensive *Jewish Cooking in America,* makes note of a "famous break-the-fast with every notable in Cincinnati attending. [According to one of the attendees:] 'Fifty percent of the people were gentiles who came and half of the Jews who came had not been to synagogue. This break-the-fast kept them within the periphery of Jewry'" (147). According to another observer of Jewish cultural trends, "Many Jews—from articulate atheists to those for whom God 'isn't really an issue'—can now attend religious ceremonies tailored to appeal to their secularized tastes and values" (Bershtel and Graubard 158).

Most of the comments about the break fast praised the emphasis on inclusivity, which extended to both the guest list as well as the observance level of the guests who attended. This might be partially due to the inevitable presence of those who are prohibited from fasting due to age or medical necessity.[7] According to a Virginia woman interviewed for a 2011 *New York Times* story on the break fast, "It's a big break-fast, . . . but it's very inclusive, in that they make an effort to invite people like us, who are new in town. And nobody ever asks whether I have fasted or not. Sometimes I bring it up, like, 'You should eat first, I didn't fast.'" When she chose to host a break fast of her own, she made a point of inviting her Muslim neighbors who were ending their Ramadan fast for the day. In the same article, Alana Newhouse, editor of the online magazine *Tablet*, admits a longstanding antipathy toward Yom Kippur. But, she claims that "ever since deciding to make a big deal out of the break-fast, the fast itself has become much more meaningful to me. There is something to look forward to, in the interaction with other Jews, and non-Jews" (Oppenheimer).

Anthropologist Carole Counihan remarks that "sharing food ensures the survival of the group both socially and materially" and this Break Fast—which as we have seen can be defined in a myriad of ways—therefore serves as a recommitment ritual for the family and the community (Counihan and Van Esterik 13). And unlike other such recommitment rituals, the break fast is more about the "good parts" of religion, without the convention and hierarchy many American Jews eschew. Parallels can be seen here to the observance of Shabbat dinners by Jews who have no intention of observing the restrictions of Shabbat or attending services on the following morning.

Amitai Etzioni's work on the modification of holidays explores the difference between edited holidays, those that are altered "on a relatively small scale," and engineered holidays, ones which are newly created (Etzioni and Bloom 30). An example of an edited Jewish holiday would be that of Chanukah, a relatively minor holiday in the Jewish calendar year that has come to be one of the more widely celebrated holidays by American Jews—mainly for reasons that have to do with the American consumer calendar. The twentieth-century creation of the *bat mitzvah* celebration can be seen either as a new life-cycle event or as an egalitarian editing of the *bar mitzvah* (Pleck 173).

But what of the break fast? The fasting itself is not edited—even though its meaning may be redefined, but the subsequent feasting is newly engineered. Joselit has suggested that the break fast might be called a "Judaized Thanksgiving," one that "seems to have grown steadily in popularity over the years, eclipsing even the fast itself" ("Breaking Down the Break Fast"). But this Judaized Thanksgiving may have come at a cost, and that cost may have been the observance of the eight-day-long Thanksgiving feast of Sukkot.

JEWISH THANKSGIVINGS

Sukkot, also known as the Festival of Booths, is celebrated as both an agricultural harvest holiday and a reminder of the Exodus. It is observed by the constructing of temporary shelters, and the commandment of "dwelling in booths" is primarily satisfied by eating in these booths. In the Jewish ritual year, the fast on Yom Kippur serves to purify the Jewish community before the subsequent "Thanksgiving" feasting of *Sukkot* which occurs several days later. Celebration of Sukkot by Jewish immigrants was well-documented at the turn of the twentieth century in America (Heinze 69). However, the observance of Sukkot has decreased (only 28 percent of American Jews claim to observe it in some way), and it appears that the break fast has stepped in to take its place (Cohen and Eisen 90).

There are several reasons why the holiday of Sukkot did not find resonance among twentieth-century Jewry. It is in some ways more helpful to first see what holidays have succeeded. Chanukah, as mentioned before, becomes widely celebrated as a Jewish alternative during the Christmas season. It was adapted for children as a result of an active campaign in the mid-twentieth century. One can "build Jewish memory through latkes" declared one Chanukah activist (Joselit, "Merry Chanuka" 315). Through food, gifts, and games, Chanukah becomes a holiday that can be celebrated with various meanings, including secular ones. Likewise, Passover (which was always a major holiday) is constantly being redefined through the publication of countless themed *haggadot* (some calling for the freedom for various oppressed peoples, or even promoting veganism as the *Haggadah for the Liberated Lamb* does).[8] Passover also, not unlike Christmas, becomes a commercial success due to the promotion of packaged food created specifically for that holiday. Twentieth-century Jewish leaders attempted to combat Jewish assimilation by any means necessary. One stealth weapon in the arsenal was *Jewish Home Beautiful*, a publication that attempted to increase religious ritual through aesthetic domesticity. Similarly, synagogue gift shops encouraged the purchase of Judaica items in order to beautify the commandments performed in the home. Ritual items such as Chanukah candelabras and Passover seder plates made perfect wedding gifts, and in addition to beautifying the home, could also be used during the associated holiday.

In contrast, while the *etrog* and *lulav* (a citron and a bundle of branches from three stipulated trees) are traditional ritual objects for Sukkot, they are both expensive and perishable. In urban Jewish neighborhoods in the early twentieth century, it was not uncommon for congregations to share these items (M. Frommer and H. Frommer 174). However, like Sabbath observance, this tradition has faded with suburbanization (Fishman 131). Additionally, the *sukkah*—the booth—involves some willingness to annually construct a temporary structure in your yard or on a balcony (for all to see). While Reform and Conservative synagogues continued to build them onsite for their congregations, congregants themselves became less likely to build individual *sukkot* at home. Restriction of immigration in the first half of the century also did away with the odder rituals in favor of those which are more in keeping with Gentile America. As Philip Roth writes of this precariously amicable relationship in his fictional midcentury town of Woodenton in "Eli the Fanatic": "For this adjustment to be made, both Jews and Gentiles alike have had to give up some of their more extreme practices in order not to threaten or offend the other" (262). Samuel G. Freedman, more than forty years later, writes of a neighborhood dispute where one Jewish couple was incensed by the erection of a *sukkah* in their next-door neighbors' front yard. "'Flaunting it' [and] 'In your face,'" complained the neighbors (15).

Nostalgia, particularly in the form of foodways, plays a big part in the retention of holidays. Unlike Passover and Chanukah, Sukkot has no notable symbolic foods. It is the *where* one eats, not the *what* that matters. Unlike Thanksgiving, a holiday menu carefully designed to reflect New England harvest traditions (even when observed in sunny California or the deserts of Utah), the best one can say is that it is good to eat "stuffed" foods on Sukkot in order to symbolize abundance. Chanukah and Passover, while filled with religious symbols, can be celebrated in a secular way that embraces American ideals of freedom. Sukkot remains purely religious. And what of its celebration of the harvest? Couldn't that be a secular entrance into this observance? In fact, Americans have a secular thanksgiving already, one which began as a religious holiday and now is happily embraced by most Americans regardless of creed.

And finally, Sukkot suffers—intentionally—from bad chronological placement. If it is too close on one end to Thanksgiving for American Jews, it is also too close on the other end to Rosh Hashanah and Yom Kippur. Even in his 1959 *Jews in Suburbia*, Albert Gordon noted that "people have grown 'weary' of the Holy Day season" and many of the moderately affiliated Jews surveyed by sociologists Steven Cohen and Arnold Eisen in the 1990s complained of a High Holiday overload by the time Sukkot arrived (Gordon 138; Cohen and Eisen). So, sadly, the holiday of Sukkot, one of the three biblical pilgrimage holidays—a holiday so important it was known in the Talmudic period as *HaChag*, *The* Holiday—has been reduced to the butt of a sitcom joke. In a contract negotiation on the television sitcom *30 Rock*, an employee requests time off for every Jewish holiday, "no matter how ridiculous." In response, his employer says that he can only have one: "What's the one where they go into the little huts?" ("Hardball"). In the context of the scene, this barb suggests that Sukkot is the most ridiculous holiday of all, and not a valued holiday worthy of time off from work. With the decrease in the observance of Sukkot, the feasting season that follows the self-denial of Yom Kippur, came the dramatically edited—if not wholly invented—break fast ritual among American Jews.

RITUAL INNOVATION AND ITS DETRACTORS

This new American break fast is certainly not without its more conservative critics, particularly the Orthodox. While Joselit suggested in a *Forward* column a few years ago that we might see the break fast "as a testament to the creative power of the grass roots and its appetite for new forms of ritual engagement. Or better yet, as an exercise in fellowship and community," an online commenter responded to her column, "My wife and I ended the Taanit on Kippur with a modest meal and juice. I've found that most of the participants in the elaborate "Break-fasts" the author described, don't even fast on Yom Ha-Kippurim to begin with!" (Joselit, "Breaking Down the Break Fast"; comment by Sephardiman). The derision shown by this disgruntled commenter is not an unusual response to new ritual—particularly in the case of those who fancy themselves the keepers of tradition. Ritually observant Jews are less likely to observe an elaborate Break Fast than their more acculturated coreligionists. In an article on the High Holidays, Steven Katz of Boston University, described the break fast as follows: "There are no special customs for breaking the fast. Rituals for this meal are a new thing. You can eat whatever you want, and usually it's only the nonreligious people who make a big deal about it. The religious Jews finish their meal, go back out, and start building the sukkah, the temporary hut used during the weeklong autumn festival of Sukkoth" (Seligson). This attitude is true on the whole for the Orthodox community—and somewhat understandable given the subsequent feasting that occurs only a few days later during Sukkot.

It is rare to find a mention of the break fast in Jewish cookbooks published under Orthodox commercial or community auspices. In what is arguably *the* most popular kosher cookbook in the first decade of the twenty-first century, the 2003 *Kosher By Design*, Susie Fishbein (the Orthodox Martha Stewart) writes: "Yom Kippur is not about food. However, eating before the fasting begins is as much of a *mitzvah* as the fast itself. It should be a full holiday meal" (70). There is no reference to a break fast at all. In the afore-mentioned *New York Times* article, she was asked about this omission and responded that she "felt it inappropriate to set up a Yom Kippur break-fast 'party,' It doesn't fit the mood of what we've done all day." Fishbein is right that Yom Kippur is not about food. Additionally, the fast that is called for requires more than just abstention from food. Other prohibited activities include bathing, sexual relations, and the wearing of leather shoes. But the emphasis on eating at the end of the day demonstrated by the break fast appears to suggest that the day is about food. After all, nobody's in a rush to hop in the shower or put their shoes back on. Fishbein does admit—albeit reluctantly—that, "It's definitely somewhat of a happy occasion. When the fast is over, the hope is that your prayers were answered, and you were written in the Book of Life and it will be a good year. So in those emotions you want to be surrounded by friends and family" (Oppenheimer).

Yet the Orthodox, despite their reputation as the standard bearers of Judaism, are a true minority among American Jews. And this new break fast ritual may very well have legs, as it is already showing signs of moving from a purely domestic celebration to one with institutional sponsorship. The *bat mitzvah*, which seemed nonsensical to many traditionalists eighty years ago, is now observed by even the strictest of Torah observers. And it is rather unlikely that Chanukah will ever again be a minor holiday in the United States. Some of these edited or engineered holidays have become so familiar that many are unaware of their novelty. In Vanessa Ochs' *Inventing Jewish Ritual*, she writes of a "*minhag* America." *Minhag* refers to a religious custom which has become so ingrained as to have the power of law. "The [Jewish] authenticity of a ritual was a feeling cultivated over time, through repeated practice, and sustained by enough cherished memories to guarantee predictability and when necessary, flexibility" (28–29, 34).

Yom Kippur is in many ways a recommitment holiday, one which employs "narratives, drama and ceremonies to directly enforce commitment to shared beliefs" (Etzioni and Bloom 11). The rituals that enforce this commitment are no longer limited to the fast and traditional liturgy. The new American break fast feast as it is now observed fills a need not just for those that are hungry after twenty-five hours of self-denial, but also for those American Jews who have been able to engage with the Jewish ritual calendar mainly through the embrace of secular symbols such as dreidels, potato pancakes, and even Chinese food. The break fast therefore embraces a symbolic ethnicity of bagels and lox in order to offer a sincerely Jewish thanksgiving (in lieu of or in addition to Sukkot) for the ability to share food with loved ones and community.

Notes

*. From *Religion, Food and Eating in North America*, edited by Benjamin E. Zeller, Marie W. Dallam, Reid L. Nelson, and Nora L. Rubel. Copyright © 2014 Columbia University Press. Reprinted with permission of the publisher.
1. See the discussion of "Sheilaism" in Bellah (221).
2. For more on fasting: Bynum; Griffith.
3. *Havdalah* is the brief ceremony marking the end of the holiday.
4. The restriction of immigration in the first half of the twentieth century leads to an ignorance of break fast rituals from the international community.
5. For a discussion of Jewish affinity for Chinese food in early twentieth-century New York, please see G. and H. L. Tuchman.
6. In August of 2011, I spent a week at the Radcliffe Institute's Culinary Collection in the Schlesinger Library. I examined ninety-eight English-language Jewish cookbooks published over the last century.
7. Jews are not obligated to fast until they have come of age (boys at age thirteen and girls at age twelve and a half). Also, pregnant women, nursing mothers, and those with medical concerns are urged to refrain from fasting.
8. *Haggadot:* plural for *haggadah,* the book that forms the basis of the Passover Seder ritual.

Works Cited

Allen, Woody, director. *Annie Hall*. United Artists, 1977.

Anshe Chesed Congregation (Cleveland Ohio) Sisterhood and Irene Rousuck. *The Fairmount Cookbook*. Cleveland, 1957.

Bellah, Robert Neelly. *Habits of the Heart: Individualism and Commitment in American Life*. Univ. of California, 1985.

Bershtel, Sara, and Allen Graubard. *Saving Remnants: Feeling Jewish in America*. Free, 1992.

"Break the Fast: A Mix-and-Match Yom Kippur Menu-Maker." *Epicurious.com*, www.epicurious.com/articlesguides/holidays/highholydays/yomkippur_recipes. Accessed 5 Oct. 2017.

Brownstein, Rita Milos, and Donna Wolf Koplowitz. *Jewish Holiday Style*. Simon & Schuster, 1999.

Bynum, Caroline Walker. *Holy Feast and Holy Fast: The Religious Significance of Food to Medieval Women*. The New Historicism: Studies in Cultural Poetics. Univ. of California, 1987.

Cohen, Jayne. *Jewish Holiday Cooking: A Food Lover's Treasury of Classics and Improvisations*. Wiley, 2008.

Cohen, Steven Martin, and Arnold M. Eisen. *The Jew Within: Self, Family, and Community in America*. Indiana Univ., 2000.

Counihan, Carole, and Penny Van Esterik. *Food and Culture: A Reader*. Routledge, 1997.

Engle, Fannie, and Gertrude Blair. *The Jewish Festival Cookbook, according to the Dietary Laws*. McKay, 1954.

Etzioni, Amitai, and Jared Bloom. *We Are What We Celebrate: Understanding Holidays and Rituals*. New York Univ., 2004.

Finch, Martha L. "Pinched with Hunger, Partaking of Plenty; Fasts and Thanksgivings in Early New England." *Eating in Eden: Food and American Utopias*, edited by Etta M. and Martha L. Finch Madden, Univ. of Nebraska, 2006, pp. 35–53.

Fishbein, Susie. *Kosher by Design: Picture-Perfect Food for the Holidays & Every Day*. 1st ed., Artscroll, 2003.

Fishman, Sylvia Barack. *Jewish Life and American Culture*. SUNY Series in American Jewish Society in the 1990s. State Univ. of New York, 2000.

Food Maven. "Breaking the Fast: Feeding the Body after Feeding the Soul." *Forward*, 26 Sept. 2003, http://forward.com/articles/8231/breaking-the-fast-feeding-the-body-after-feeding/. Accessed 5 Oct. 2017.

Freedman, Samuel G. *Jew Vs. Jew: The Struggle for the Soul of American Jewry*. Simon & Schuster, 2000.

Frommer, Myrna, and Harvey Frommer. *Growing up Jewish in America: An Oral History*. 1st ed., Harcourt Brace, 1995.

Gans, Herbert J. "Symbolic Ethnicity: The Future of Ethnic Groups and Cultures in America." *Ethnic and Racial Studies*, vol. 2, 1979, pp. 1–20.

Goldstein, Joyce Esersky. *Sephardic Flavors: Jewish Cooking of the Mediterranean.* Chronicle Books, 2000.

———. *Saffron Shores: Jewish Cooking of the Southern Mediterranean.* Chronicle Books, 2002.

Gordon, Albert Isaac. *Jews in Suburbia.* Beacon, 1959.

Greenberg, Irving. *The Jewish Way: Living the Holidays.* Aronson, 1998.

Griffith, R. Marie. *Born Again Bodies: Flesh and Spirit in American Christianity.* California Studies in Food and Culture 12. Univ. of California, 2004.

Grossinger, Jennie. *The Art of Jewish Cooking.* Random House, 1958.

"Hardball." *30 Rock*, created by Tina Fey, season 1, episode 15, NBC, 2007.

Heinze, Andrew R. *Adapting to Abundance: Jewish Immigrants, Mass Consumption, and the Search for American Identity.* Columbia History of Urban Life. Columbia Univ., 1990.

Joselit, Jenna Weissman. "Breaking Down the Break Fast." *Forward*, 3 Oct. 2007, www.forward.com/articles/11731/. Accessed 5 Oct. 2017.

———. "Merry Chanuka: The Changing Holiday Practices of American Jews, 1880–1950." *The Uses of Tradition: Jewish Continuity in the Modern Era*, edited by Jack Wertheimer, Jewish Theological Seminary of America, 1992, pp. 303–05.

———. *The Wonders of America: Reinventing Jewish Culture 1880–1950.* 1st ed., Hill and Wang, 1994.

Kirshenblatt-Gimblett, Barbara. "Kitchen Judaism." *Getting Comfortable in New York: The American Jewish Home, 1880–1950*, edited by Jenna Weissman Joselit and Susan L. Braunstein. Jewish Museum, 1990.

Levi, Shonie B., and Sylvia R. Kaplan. *Guide for the Jewish Homemaker.* 2nd rev. ed., National Women's League of the United Synagogue of America, 1964.

Nathan, Joan. *Jewish Cooking in America.* Expanded ed., Knopf Cooks American. Knopf, 1998.

Ochs, Vanessa. *Inventing Jewish Ritual.* 1st ed., Jewish Publication Society, 2007.

Oppenheimer, Mark. "Traditional Meal Ending Holy Days Becomes an Event." *New York Times*, 1 Oct. 2011.

Pew Forum on Religion & Public Life. "U. S. Religious Landscape Survey." Edited by Pew Research Center, Pew Research Center, 2008.

Pleck, Elizabeth Hafkin. *Celebrating the Family Ethnicity, Consumer Culture, and Family Rituals.* Harvard Univ., 2000.

Roth, Philip. "Eli the Fanatic." *Goodbye, Columbus, and Five Short Stories*, edited by Philip Roth, Houghton Mifflin, 1959.

Seligson, Susan. "In Days of Awe, Rituals Sweet and Somber: Steven Katz Walks Us through High Holy Days." *BU Today*, 8 Sept. 2010, www.bu.edu/today/node/11462. Accessed 5 Oct. 2017.

Sephardiman. 9 Oct. 2007.

Sirkis, Ruth. *A Taste of Tradition: The How and Why of Jewish Gourmet Holiday Cooking.* Ritchie, 1972.

Sklare, Marshall, and Joseph Greenblum. *Jewish Identity on the Suburban Frontier: A Study of Group Survival in the Open Society*. Lakeville Studies, vol. 1. Basic Books, 1967.

Sneiderman, Marilyn. "Home and Work, Community and Advocacy." *ZEEK: A Jewish Journal of Thought and Culture*, 11 Nov. 2010, zeek.forward.com/articles/117056/. Accessed 5 Oct. 2017.

Tuchman, Gaye and Harry Levine. "New York Jews and Chinese Food: The Social Construction of an Ethnic Pattern." *Journal of Contemporary Ethnography*, vol. 22, 1993, pp. 382–407.

United Jewish Communities. "The National Jewish Population Survey 2000–01." New York, 2003.

Eating My Way through *Transparent*

by Rebecca T. Alpert

The first three seasons of Amazon's award winning series *Transparent* have been heralded and dissected by scholars for their incredibly sophisticated presentation of both religious and cultural Judaism as practiced (or not) in contemporary America. One way that creator Jill Soloway's series reveals and illustrates the Jewish world

The Official Poster for Season 2 (Courtesy of Amazon Content Services LLC)

of the main protagonists, the Pfefferman family, is through their relationship to Jewish foodways. Each family member ("transparent" Maura, their[1] ex-wife Shelley, and the adult offspring Sarah, Josh, and Allie) expresses their character's personalities, joys, pain, and longings not only through the show's dominant modality of sexuality, but also significantly through what they do—and do not—eat both together and individually. Food takes a prominent role on both daily and ritual occasions that are marked as Jewish and not-Jewish. As Carol Harris-Shapiro suggests, the turn away from the institutional and towards familial and individual spiritual expressions of Jewishness is reflected in how Jews eat. The Pfeffermans provide a rich example of this development in American religious life (Harris-Shapiro).

What the Pfeffermans do with food—eating together in key moments, recognizing the Jewish roots of their eating habits, using meals as occasions both to celebrate joy and experience/express deprivation and confusion—will be central to each of their stories. Collectively, their foodways represent their identity as Jewish Americans, both through their assimilation into and simultaneously standing apart from an American mainstream culture. The effortless way they employ food—cooking, eating, sharing, disdaining—both at key moments of family sanctity and as individuals wrestling with competing impulses—reveals surprising details of American Jewish values, concerns and anxieties. The exaggerations of each character—expressed by their consumption and production of food—operate as a way of exploring and expressing cultural norms and expectations. And they illustrate generational changes in perceptions not only about food but also gender, transition, and sexuality; the Pfefferemans normalize and enfold seeming atypical or non-normative "sexways" just as they have foodways. Each member of the family uses Jewish food to express their personalities, their relationship to Judaism and each other. As a whole, *Transparent* uses food as a means to illustrate how cultural Jews experience American Jewish life. The food practices of the main characters help us understand the key role eating Jewishly has in the familial and personal Judaism so central to American Jewish life today, indicate how those foodways are tied to the Jewish past, and raise doubts about whether this type of Jewish identity can sustain itself in the future.

FAMILY DINNER

The family name Pfefferman [Pepper-man] may be derived from the German occupational term for spice traders,[2] which marks the connection to food at their family's core. Beginning in the pilot episode eating exemplifies how each character defines their relationships to the world, to their Jewishness, and to each other. Siblings Allie and Josh have breakfast together while she teases him about the young singing group he's managing, suggesting that he get them children's food, "juice boxes and string cheese" which is her way of pointing out how inappropriate she thinks that relationship is. Maura tries (and fails) to tell her children about their transition over a shared dinner that Sarah brings to her father's house. When Maura compliments her on how perfect the take out meal is, Sarah suggests that on her tombstone it will say, "she always knew how much to order." During the course of the meal Allie describes her efforts to be gluten-free which marks the first of many efforts she will make to find the right way to relate to eating as she figures out her relationship to herself, her family, and Judaism. Josh and Maura (at that point, Morty) eat barbecued ribs with great relish, as Allie and Sarah joke about how messy the "men" are with barbecue sauce staining their faces and clothes. Josh complains that their parents never taught them how to eat properly. Maura responds, that's because they are *shtetl* people. "Your grandma Rose actually ate lettuce with her bare hands." Later in the episode, Allie arrives at her mother's, welcomed by the words, "I'm going to cut up cantaloupe," a food fit for diets that they eat together as they talk about what might be going on with Maura. At the episode's end, Allie meets a personal trainer who asks her about her food habits. What she describes as deprivation, he redefines for her as discipline. But disciplined eating is not a cultural Jewish approach, and Allie cannot sustain it.

Their foodways are not based on Jewish law, but Ashkenazi American custom. Food and food practices are divided not by kosher and *treif* but by Jewish and "goyish." All of the Pfeffermans encounter and mock or are alienated from food that, as Lenny Bruce would have it, is "goyish"—what Christians, not Jews, would eat. At Idyllwild Womyn's Festival, Maura, Sarah, and Allie joke about the politically correct (and inedible) nut loaf and tofu dogs. Allie finds herself deeply disturbed by the fantasies she has of a hyper-masculine transman who drinks Pabst Blue Ribbon beer. Josh's son Colton's Christian family serves corn on the cob and deviled eggs, and Maura's grandparents disdain Waldorf Salad as not Jewish. It is central to the Pfeffermans' existence that they eat like Jews. Note that none of these alien foods is traditionally "*treif*"; a Jew keeping kosher could eat all of them and many have.

Jews do drink beer and eat Waldorf salad and deviled eggs. And many a Jewish vegetarian has adopted nutloaf for Shabbat dinner. Much of the food that is culturally Jewish to the Pfeffermans—from the barbecued ribs to the frequent containers of Chinese food that appear—is most likely not kosher at all. But the Pfeffermans' Jewishness is cultural. The boundaries are self-defined and intuitive, as are those that Lenny Bruce described in the 1960s.[3] As Tuchman and Levine suggest, American Jews, like other ethnic groups, create their own ethnicity by fusing elements of tradition and innovation in their eating practices (See Tuchman and Levine).

In the first episode and throughout all three seasons, the older generation, Maura and Shelley, are distinguished by their connections to an imagined Jewish culinary past. Maura's ancestry and childhood foodways are marked as part of Ashkenazi/Eastern European Jewish traditions; she exposes more of a style of eating (with gusto rather than gentility) than the actual foodstuffs being imbibed. Shelley's eating habits represent the next generation; she wittingly and unwittingly demonstrates the children of immigrants' desire for suburban assimilation, the dream of becoming the svelte version of a "Jewish mother" who cares more about maintaining her figure than eating with gusto. Their children in turn provide a different set of contemporary food-constructed identity politics. Sarah expresses her ambivalence towards her mother's suburban Jewishness by carving out her own version of Jewish and maternal eating marked by the absence of home cooking. Josh comes to represent male gustatory pleasure in a complicated dance with traditional Jewish foodways that provide psychological outlets for his grief and consolation. And Allie works through her shifting queer Jewish identity in relation to Jewish (and queer) food rituals that celebrate and question Jewish familial practices.

MAURA

Even while eating barbecued ribs that mark their food practices as outside the bounds of observant Jewish behavior and traditional Jewish eating based in the laws of *kashrut*, Maura asserts their family Jewish roots as "*shtetl* people"; she jokes about their ancestry with self-deprecating, absurd humor. Maura is their link to their European Jewish past; she is a child of survivors of Hitler's Germany. Ironically, the Pfeffermans' German Jewish roots are not at all "*shtetlach*." German Jews like the Pfeffermans were thoroughly assimilated to

German cultural practices and either unaware of or alienated from the Eastern European foodways that Maura claims as her own. (Perhaps that is why it was lettuce her mother ate with her bare hands.[4])

But in America, Jews were perceived as all coming from Eastern Europe, and it is those traditions that the *Transparent* writers adopt.[5] Living with her grandparents in 1950s America, Maura imbibes their notions of comfort food that her *zayde* (Haim) claims will preserve them and keep them safe in the fall-out shelter as they anticipate the nuclear apocalypse: chocolate, pickles, canned tuna. When the table talk turns to ideas of heaven, her grandmother Yetta scoffs at Christian ideas Maura tells them her friends have, suggesting to her mockingly that she "go eat a Waldorf Salad" if that is her religious preference.

It is her cultural connection to these Jewish ancestors that defines her and is symbolized here through her relationship to Jewish eating. We may be eating *treif*, her words imply, but we eat Jewishly nonetheless, because we are *shtetl* people and eating with gusto, i.e., without "gentile" manners, comes naturally to us. It is that sensibility that Maura wants to bring to her experience of gender transition—that while queer may be *treif* it is still very natural and very Jewish. As an adult Maura no longer practices religious Judaism and is often portrayed as the outsider in ritual scenes.[6] But she creates her own Jewish food ritual by telling her biofamily and her chosen family of transfolk about wanting to undergo gender confirmation surgery over birthday cake for her seventieth birthday. Thus, food supports Maura's "queerness"—not just an expression of the fluidity of identities but also the conduit for the transition between them.

SHELLEY

While Maura never offers food or cooks like a stereotypically good suburban American Jewish mother, Shelley performs that role. Offering Allie cantaloupe and eating this low calorie fruit often found on diets in the 1950s with her evokes the desires of suburban Jewish women to overcome the stereotype of the food-centric Jewish mother by blending in and staying slim (see Antler; Thompson 35–37). Just as Shelley's first act involves greeting her daughter with food, she is often found by an open refrigerator, noshing diet food. She drinks diet soda and vitamin water. She does perform one aspect of the prototypical "good Jewish mother" in her preoccupation with offering food to others, as when she obsesses over bringing a sufficient quantity of mustard to her second husband Ed's funeral. Unlike the other Pfeffermans, and as one would expect from the Jewish mother stereotype, she rarely eats full meals herself. In the flashback to when she first met Mort, we find young Shelley in a 1960s-style diner. The opening scene depicts the delights available in that place: chocolate cake, coke, French fries, triple-decker sandwiches, meringue pies. The other diners eat while Shelley and her friend Deb abstemiously drink coffee. Looking to find herself through others, the adult and now divorced Shelley finds herself attracted to Buzz, a man with a large appetite. When they invite Shelley's children over, Buzz grills rare (bloody) meat, and Shelley jokes about loving not only Buzz's grilling skills but also Buzz's meat, one of the few instances where foodways boldly cross over into the realm of the sexual to accentuate Shelley's efforts to climb out of her abstemious nature. Buzz entices her to the take the family on a cruise by describing the raw bar buffet's delights: clams, oysters, shrimp, and "scallops the size of footballs." Although she meets Buzz in synagogue where he is an active member, the foods he eats mark him both as a lover of *treif* and as Shelley's opposite in terms of appetite. It is this difference between Shelley, the good Jewish mother and Buzz, who in Yiddish would be the "*fresser*," that dooms their relationship. Shelley's foodways expose both her desire to be noticed and her halting knowledge of how to express herself through her desire to connect with her family through food. At Maura's seventieth birthday party she proclaims "the kitchen is the heart of the home." But food—and nourishment—seem to be something for them and not for her. She is the quintessential Jewish mother/martyr of the generation of Jewish suburban women.

SARAH

Sarah is the next generation's version of Shelley; now the ambivalent Jewish mother. Her relationship to food is mostly understated. Her mother's suburban American Jewish "good Jewish mother" food practices are something she wants to leave behind. She feels conflicted about her own legacy relating to similarities to her mother, but is comfortable in the role of the next generation's version of Jewish (if not good/nurturing) motherhood: she is a fully assimilated suburban lady who knows how to order take-out. Sarah's explorations of lesbianism, BDSM, and polyamory are efforts to break out of that role and, to a great extent, she succeeds. Of all the members of the Pfefferman clan her connections to food are the least elaborately portrayed; her hungers are explored and satisfied sexually. While all the ritual occasions the family celebrates are marked by eating, there is no food shown at Sarah and Tammy's wedding. When Tammy displays her anger at Sarah by leaving her at a subsequent pool party and throwing their wedding cake into the pool, Sarah's rejection of food is mirrored in a rejection of other appetites. Despite herculean efforts, she cannot get out from under her mother's model for the good Jewish mother who gives without taking.

When Sarah reunites with her Christian husband Len, her return to suburban (but not Jewish) motherhood is symbolized by cooking a dinner for him that includes salad and zucchini blossoms, to which he responds jokingly, "what have you done with my wife?" Her other effort at normalcy—she attempts to fit in at the synagogue—also involves inventing a Tacos con Torah night, but she ends up serving papusas. In her lack of understanding of Jewish traditions, she is perplexed by the rabbi's consternation about the change in menu (and alliteration) and, in playing ignorant, she exposes a continued lack of concern about Jewish terminology (and Judaic accuracy) when she suggests they can call it Papusas con Psalms instead. In her search for authenticity, she reveals a disconcerting ability to offer substitutions that lack consistency or integrity; tacos or spouses, sexuality or salad, Sarah attempts to fill gaps in her self-understanding without investing in a search for meaning or connection to her Jewish heritage.

JOSH

Josh's messily digging into his *treif* barbecue with abandon in the pilot episode characterizes the way he copes with his desires and sorrows. Josh uses food as he does sex; he seeks from them both pleasure and solace. He would not distinguish "Jewish" from "goyish," either in his choice of partners, family, or food. He spends much time in the kitchen and is seen cooking and eating more often than any of the other family members. His diet consists primarily of breakfast foods like eggs, pancakes, cereal. Yet Josh's food habits—especially when shown at critical, emotionally laden moments—are intimately though negatively tied to *kashrut*; he breaks taboos at acute junctures. After his stepfather Ed's funeral and *shiva* service, the family sits down to dinner. Immediately prior to the meal, Josh learns that he has a son, now a teenager, with and from the Pfefferman children's childhood nanny Rita. Colton joins the family to eat. An observant Christian, Colton differentiates himself by refusing to eat the quintessentially Ashkenazi Jewish food, chopped liver. He also wants to say a prayer before the meal. Josh responds reactively, "We're Jews. We don't," although of course religious Jews would recite the blessing over the meal, *hamotzi*. Josh's relationship to Judaism may be tangentially connected to its cultural foodways, but not in any way to the prayers that accompany those foods at a more traditional Jewish table. Seeking Colton out after his return to the Christian family who adopted him, Josh shucks corn and eats deviled eggs thereby marking his desire to be part of a non-Jewish world. But he cannot escape his Jewish roots completely.

Josh is also drawn to Judaism through his on and off romance with the family's rabbi, Raquel. After breaking up with Raquel the first time, and enduring an agonizing Yom Kippur in and out of synagogue, Josh attends Allie's family dinner to break the Yom Kippur fast. But what he experiences (the revelation about his son through the secret sexual ties to his nanny Rita when he was young; the break-up with Raquel and the miscarriage that preceded it) is unbearable. He cannot bring himself to join the family to break the fast he had not been keeping. Maura offers to trade bagels (his pumpernickel for her everything), but unlike on so many other occasions, he refuses food and announces that Raquel has miscarried their child and he has ended their relationship. In that moment food can neither offer solace nor solve his confusion. Yet the episode ends with Josh once again finding in food a way to cope with his loss. He walks the aisle of a supermarket and attempts to deal with his grief by tearing open and devouring (*treif*) lunch meats and bread. He finds some relief as he *shtupps* them violently into his mouth. Breaking taboos with food (both eating in the supermarket and eating *treif*) is his mechanism to cope with his sadness. Unlike the other Pfeffermans, Josh has a powerful relationship to Jewish food taboos. While the others may do it casually, he eats *treif* with zeal and the gusto that Maura understood as the hallmark of Jewish eating. Like the others in his family, Josh uses food not only to express his identity but to cope with his life problems.

Later, in season two, Josh is still trying to deal with his sadness. Waking up he goes to make himself eggs for breakfast. But when he discovers the first one is bloody, he puts it aside and has cereal instead, unconsciously observing the religious taboo against eating blood. Walking to the pool he finds his sisters. Bonding over stories of their childhood they re-enact an underwater tea party, pretending to eat and drink together, in harmony.

In season 3 Josh and Allie still live (and frequently cook) together in their childhood home. Sarah confesses to Allie her jealousy of the closeness Josh and Allie have, suggesting that she stole Josh away from her, the big sister, the minute Allie was born into the family. And what does she resent most that they are they doing now? Baking cakes together. Her perception is confirmed later in that episode when Josh and Allie connect over eating pancakes and sausage patties Josh has prepared; as they share breakfast for supper, they exhibit a special bond that is sealed by food.

Josh's relationship to Jewish foodways is complex. He unconsciously plays with Jewish food taboos, both breaking and observing rules of *kashrut* he does not know (like throwing away a bloody egg) and so can only be presumed to represent his "biogenetic" Jewishness. But he, more than any other Pfefferman, uses food to mitigate pain and anguish. While others drink to solve their problems, like a good Jew, Josh eats. With gusto.

ALLIE

As noted above, Allie and Josh frequently appear eating together which becomes a visual symbol of their deep sibling connection. In contrast to Josh's eating as emotional consolation however, Allie seeks to discover life's meaning through her food practices. Eating is part of Allie's process of finding her place in the world as a queer Jewish woman; it also defines and demarcates her relationship with her family members. The pilot began with Allie teasing Josh about food he should provide for his young musicians and about his barbecue mess, explaining to Maura, Josh, and Sarah her gluten-free eating, and receiving Shelley's abstemious love by way of the cut up cantaloupe.

In the next episode we find Allie and Josh at Canter's, the famous Los Angeles Jewish delicatessen on Fairfax. This pilgrimage to this shrine to Ashkenazi Jewish eating marks this family as part of the traditional Ashkenazi world of Los Angeles Jewry. As Sarah brought food to her father's house in the episode before, Josh and Allie bring food to eat at their mother's. The camera pans the food cases filled with smoked fish, deli meats and cheesecakes as a reminder that eating Jewish is being Jewish for the Pfefferman family. Sister and brother discuss Josh's sex life and Allie's food life, as she requests that the counterman give her a sample the "tofu schmeer" as a cream cheese substitute for her newly-discovered commitment to eating dairy-free as ordained by her personal trainer. Because they are picking up Shelley's "standing order" Josh worries that their mother will be upset at the addition of tofu cream cheese, but Allie dismisses his concern. Allie's dairy-free regimen only lasts as long as the relationship with the personal trainer; by episode six she buys an ice cream cone while walking with Josh, who chides her about being back on dairy. Compared to the rest of her family, Allie's relationship to food is not stable. As she tries on different queer Jewish identities, her foodways shift accordingly.

The most important contribution Allie makes to understanding the Pfefferman's culinary Jewish life is in her role as the family's ritual organizer. What Rabbi Raquel is to institutional Judaism, Allie is to the Pfefferman's familial version of Jewishness. Jewish food rituals have always centered on the family unit and taken place in the home more than the synagogue. Despite their thoroughly unorthodox ways, the Pfeffermans are deeply connected to the cultural codes of American Jewish practices. In two key episodes Allie, like many contemporary liberal rabbis, is a ritual creator. She invents Pfefferman-specific food rituals to correspond to significant moments on the Jewish calendar and mark key moments in their collective lives. In season two she hosts a family Yom Kippur break-the-fast with her then girlfriend Syd. And at the conclusion of season three she creates an impromptu Seder on the cruise the five Pfeffermans, then all single again, are taking together at their mother's behest. It is these two events that reveal how Jewish rituals survive in a cultural context even when devoid of/passed beyond religious meaning. Allie barely knows how to make these rituals. She relies on Syd's knowledge on Yom Kippur and some deeply seated childhood memories to provide the cruise Seder. Yet she understands intuitively the deeply needed ritual that helps her family transition from one emotional space to another, thus keeping Jewishness alive through her improvisations.

For their break-the-fast, Syd and Allie cook all day to make food for their families at the end of Yom Kippur. As they cook they lament how hard it is to make food while fasting. Allie begins to have food fantasies in which everything starts to look like food. As the guests arrive they are told that they are not being served water in solidarity with the California state drought, but wine and skim milk would be available. In this, Allie is integrating her queer political sensibility into their Jewish food practices.[7] In keeping with Jewish tradition, they eat dairy—warm blintzes and Canter's famous cole slaw. Allie leads the ritual, contextualizing the meal in relation to the theme of the holiday of Yom Kippur—forgiveness—as she requests that they reveal what they have atoned for. They say *hamotzi*, the blessing thanking God for the bread (the same one that Josh told Colton at Ed's *shiva* that Jews do not say before eating). Allie then continues her leadership role, encouraging them to hold their bagels aloft, and Shelley's new boyfriend Buzzy helps them remember the words of the prayer that they sing cacophonously together. As ritual leader, Allie attempts to bring her family together. Traditional Ashkenazi foods for the break-the-fast (bagels, blintzes, cole slaw), are necessary to maintain a connection to Jewish tradition, while the ritual of revealing what one needs to atone for is quite outside the bounds of normative religious practice. In Allie's ritual, food, not prayer, connects the Pfeffermans to their Jewishness.

Allie's greatest ritual moment occurs as the climax to season three. The five Pfeffermans, all without partners, find themselves alone together on a cruise. The episode takes place on the eighth day of Passover, and Allie, in her capacity as the family's Jewish ritual organizer/rabbi, feels the need for a ritual to unite them. Completely outside any normative Ashkenazi religious practice, she cobbles together a ceremony that she calls a Seder.[8] She and Sarah scout out the elements that belong on the Seder plate. With amazing accuracy and inventiveness, and without any regard for traditional *kashrut* or Passover restrictions on *hametz* (leavened bread), they raid the buffet to assemble a shank bone (after eating the meat on it), greens for parsley, wasabi to stand in for bitter herbs, saltines for matzah, an egg, and a fabulous concoction of raisins, nuts, and balsamic vinegar for the *haroset*. Allie makes the Hillel sandwich—*haroset* on saltines—and asks each of them to take a bite and say from what they want to be freed, echoing her ritual practice of asking her family to reveal what they were atoning for on Yom Kippur. But this time the ritual works and each member of the family is able to articulate their needs. Josh names his desire to be freed from this ritual and from this family, and he leaves. In his misery, Jewish family food rituals are not the answer he seeks for his pain. Maura, who unlike her son finds that the Seder ritual meets her needs, speaks of her desire to be rid of the shame, pain, and fear that have haunted her process of transition. Shelley also responds, telling them that she will be performing her story later, because Trevor, "the gay who comes with her room" believes in her artistic abilities. While the Jewish ritual does not work for her in the moment, it is her chance to tell the family that she will indeed find her voice in this other medium. At the same time her response is very Jewish. She further explains that from Trevor she also "gets a poached egg on demand." Shelley's simple desires (to be listened to, to be served a poached egg) are reminiscent of the Yiddish tale of Bontsha the Silent, who, after suffering incredible indignities on earth is offered anything he wants in heaven, and asks for a warm roll with butter. In naming their respective experiences of personal and emotional enslavement, each of the Pfeffermans enact the commandment most associated with Passover: they tell their own—and their collective—story. Thus, the ritual meal on the cruise mimics the journey of the Exodus memory but in a unique and utterly narcissistic way.

CONCLUSION

Jewish food practices, both religiously and culturally-based, are important signposts in the lives of the secular Jewish Pfeffermans. The spices that they eponymously trade give us a powerful picture of how they see themselves as American Jews. We take (with a grain of salt) that they are comfortably assimilated. Yet they clearly long to "spice up" their American lives with somewhat idiosyncratic connections to their Jewishness through their foodways. They avoid ways of eating that set Jews apart, defying traditionally regulated *kashrut* and eschewing abstemious suburban Jewish mother behavior of generations past. Their most poignant moments together are arguably eating in ways that are at turns comforting, celebratory, and odd, both at the break-the-fast and at the ersatz Seder. Individually, their foodways mirror their hopes for themselves as American Jews. The older Pfeffermans ate with gusto (Maura) yet simply (Shelley). Sarah, Josh and Allie translate those patterns into American Jewish foodways that are both traditional and bizarre: Canter's cole slaw and tofu shmeer; eggs without blood and supermarket deli meats, Papusas con Psalms and coffee beans from Israel; hard boiled eggs and saltines for matzah on Passover. What is absent (and remains to be seen) is what the next generation of American Jewish living and eating will look like. Neither Sarah's young children nor Josh's Christian son offer any clues.

Transparent uses Jewish foodways to expose, explore and analyze the current state of secular American Jewish life. It illustrates how non-observant Ashkenazi Jews connect to their Jewish past through memory, nostalgia, constructed meaning, and food. It informs the viewers—Jews and non-Jews—about the difficulties and creative energies they use to live a Jewish life. Jewish food practices—what is consumed, when it is consumed, and why it is consumed—take the place of institutional Judaism. On one hand, the loss of one anchor—a denominationally defined Jewish community—indicates that this family lacks a blueprint for Jewish behavior; on the other hand, food presents a type of continuity that will sustain them in the next generation.

Notes

1. I use the plural "they" here to signal the grammatical limitations of the two gender options "his/her."
2. Pfefferman is a common German Jewish patronymic that may have been based on occupation, but there is no conclusive evidence to verify the authenticity of that claim. Perhaps Soloway was looking for a German name, or perhaps she had something more in mind related to the family as purveyors of a new kind of "spicy" American Jewish identity. (On the origin of Jewish family names, see H. W. and E. H. Guggenheimer 585).
3. Lenny Bruce's comedy routine from the mid-1960s drew distinctions between Jews and non-Jews. He recorded several different versions and, of course, varied the comparisons when he performed the routine live. In his very thorough and compelling study of the role Jewishness and Judaism played in Bruce's comedic output, David Kaufman quotes this version: "Dig. I'm Jewish. . . . Koolaid is *goyish.* All Drake's Cakes are *goyish.* Pumpernickel is Jewish, and, as you know, white bread is very *goyish.* Instant potatoes-*goyish.* Black cherry soda's very Jewish. Macaroons are *very* Jewish—very Jewish cake. Fruit salad is Jewish. Lime jello is *goyish.* Lime soda is *very goyish*" (123). Kaufman quotes Cohen (31) and compares it to recorded versions on *Lenny Bruce: Let The Buyer Beware*, disc 3, cut 17 and disc 5, cut 6.
4. Tuchman and Levine point out that German Jews were not involved in the American Jewish assimilatory strategy of eating Chinese food, for example (399).
5. It is not only German Jewish eating patterns that are left out of the story; the Ashkenazi/Eastern European-centric stereotype ignores the foodways of the twenty percent of American Jewry that is Sephardic, Mizrachi, or from the Maghreb.
6. It is Maura who inappropriately inserts *Kaddish* at *Havdalah*, cannot comfortably take her role as a candle-lighting Jewish mother, mixes up Chanukah and Shabbat tunes she learned as a child, and performs *tashlich* on Yom Kippur rather than Rosh Hashanah by casting bread to geese as atonement for her sins.
7. The only other time politics enters, also in relation to food, is in Season 3 when Leslie, Allie's feminist girlfriend/Women's Studies instructor, gets into an argument with congregants at the Papusa con Psalms event at the synagogue. Leslie refuses espresso made from Sinai coffee beans from Israel because she boycotts Israeli products to support Palestinian rights.
8. Moroccan Jews do observe a communal ritual meal, Maimuna, on the eighth (and final) night of the holiday of Passover ("Passover: Maimuna").

Works Cited

Antler, Joyce. *You Never Call! You Never Write!: A History of the Jewish Mother.* Oxford Univ., 2007.

Cohen, John, editor. *The Essential Lenny Bruce.* Bell, 1970.

Guggenheimer, Heinrich W. and Eva H. *Jewish Family Names and Their Origins: An Etymological Dictionary.* KTAV, 1992.

Harris-Shapiro, Carol. "Bloody Shankbones and Braided Bread: The Food Voice and the Fashioning of American Jewish Identities." *Food & Foodways*, vol. 14, 2006, pp. 67–90.

Kaufman, David. *Jewhooing the Sixties: American Celebrity and Jewish Identity.* Brandeis Univ., 2012.

Lenny Bruce: Let the Buyer Beware. Shout! Factory, 5 Oct. 1961, disc 3, cut 17.

———. Shout! Factory, Nov. 1961, disc 5, cut 6.

"Passover: Maimuna." *Jewish Virtual Library*, www.jewishvirtuallibrary.org/maimuna. Accessed 17 Aug. 2017.

Thompson, Becky. *A Hunger So Wide and So Deep: American Women Speak Out on Eating Problems.* Univ. of Minnesota, 1994.

Tuchman, Gaye, and Harry Gene Levine. "New York Jews and Chinese Food: An Ethnic Construction of a Social Pattern." *Journal of Contemporary Ethnography*, vol. 22, no. 3, 1993, pp. 382–407.

About the Contributors

REBECCA T. ALPERT is Professor of Religion and Senior Associate Dean in the College of Liberal Arts at Temple University. She attended Barnard College before receiving her PhD in religion at Temple University and her rabbinical training at the Reconstructionist Rabbinical College in Wyncote, Pennsylvania. After spending the early part of her career in academic administration, Alpert joined the faculty at Temple University in 1997 in the department of Religion and the Women's Studies program. She is the co-author of *Exploring Judaism: A Reconstructionist Approach*, author of *Like Bread on the Seder Plate: Jewish Lesbians and the Transformation of Tradition* and *Whose Torah? A Concise Guide to Progressive Judaism*. Her recent scholarship examines religion and sports. *Out of Left Field: Jews and Black Baseball*, was published by Oxford University Press in June 2011. *Religion and Sport: An Introduction and Case Studies*, was published by Columbia University Press in 2015. She is currently co-editing an anthology, *Gods, Games, and Globalization* (with Arthur Remillard) to be published by Mercer University Press. Alpert received the Christian R. and Mary F. Lindback Teaching Award (2013) and Temple University's Great Teacher Award (2016).

LISA ANSELL is Associate Director of the Casden Institute for the Study of the Jewish Role in American Life at the University of Southern California. She received her BA in French and Near East Studies from UCLA and her MA in Middle East Studies from Harvard University. She was the Chair of the World Language Department of New Community Jewish High School for five years before coming to USC in August, 2007. She currently teaches Hebrew language courses at the Hebrew Union College-Jewish Institute of Religion.

HASIA DINER is the Paul and Sylvia Steinberg Professor of American Jewish History and Professor of Hebrew in the Skirball Department of Hebrew and the Department of History at New York University. Her areas of research interest include American Jewish history, American immigration history, and women's history, and her honors have included the Guggenheim Fellowship and Fellow of the American Academy of Jewish Research. Dr. Diner's recent publications include *Roads Taken: The Great Jewish Migrations to the New World and the Peddlers Who Forged the Way* (Yale University, 2015) and *We Remember with Reverence and Love: American Jews and the Myth of Silence after the Holocaust, 1945–1962* (New York University, 2009), winner of the National Jewish Book Award and the Saul Viener Prize.

LEAH HOCHMAN directs the Jerome H. Louchheim School for Judaic Studies at the University of Southern California and is associate professor of Jewish Thought at the Hebrew Union College-Jewish Institute of Religion in Los Angeles. She received her BA from Pitzer College and her MA and PhD in religion and literature from Boston University. She has been a fellow at the Moses Mendelssohn Zentrum in Potsdam, the Oxford Centre for Hebrew and Jewish Studies, the Simon Dubnow Institute in Leipzig, and the Einstein Forum in Potsdam. She taught previously at the University of Florida and Boston University. Her book *The Ugliness of Moses Mendelssohn: Aesthetics, Religion, and Morality in the Eighteenth Century* was published by Routledge in 2014.

EVE JOCHNOWITZ, Yiddish instructor at the YIVO institute and the Workmen's Circle, has been teaching Yiddish Language, Culture, and Literature, as well as Yiddish Foodways and Dance for twenty-five years. She worked for several years as a cook and baker in New York and received her PhD in Jewish culinary ethnography in the Department of Performance Studies from New York University. She has lectured both in the United States and abroad on food in Jewish tradition, religion, and ritual as well as food in Yiddish performance and popular culture. She blogs in English and Yiddish at inmolaraan.blogspot.com and is the co-host with Rukhl Schaechter Ejdelman, of *Est Gezunterheyt!*, a cooking show in Yiddish. The *Vilna Vegetarian Cookbook*, translated, annotated, and adapted for the modern kitchen, was published in 2015. Dr. Jochnowitz is the chocolate lady.

JEFFREY A. MARX's publications on the the history of cream cheese in America include: "Philadelphia® Comes to New York: The Marketing of Cream Cheese in New York State," in *New York History, Quarterly Journal of the New York State Historical Association and The State University of New York College at Oneonta*, vol. 96, no. 2 (2015); and "The Days Had Come of Curds and Cream: The Origins and Development of Cream Cheese in America, 1870–1880," in *Food, Culture & Society*, vol. 15, no. 2 (2012). He is currently working on the history of Breakstone Bros. Dairy of New York.

DEBORAH R. PRINZ's book, *On the Chocolate Trail: A Delicious Adventure Connecting Jews, Religions, History, Travel, Rituals and Recipes to the Magic of Cacao* (2nd edition, 2017) is being used in adult study, classroom settings, book clubs and chocolate tastings. She co-curates the "Jews on the Chocolate Trail" exhibit for the Herbert and Eileen Bernard Museum of Temple Emanu-El, New York City. It features historical and contemporary art, artifacts and memorabilia that portray stories of Jews and chocolate. She was awarded a Starkoff Fellowship and a Director's Fellowship from the American Jewish Archives as well as a Gilder Lehrman Fellowship from the Rockefeller Library to research the book. Prinz lectures about chocolate and religion around the world and blogs at onthechocolatetrail.org, the *Huffington Post*, the *Forward* and the *Jewish Journal*. Rabbi Prinz has held a number of leadership positions in the national and regional Reform movement, having served the Central Conference of American Rabbis (CCAR) as Director of Program and Member Services and the Director of the Joint Commission on Rabbinic Mentoring. Prior to that, she was a congregational rabbi for close to thirty years.

STEVEN J. ROSS is Professor of History at the University of Southern California, and Myron and Marian Director of the Casden Institute for the Study of the Jewish Role in American Life. He is the author of *Working-Class Hollywood: Silent Film and the Shaping of Class in America* (Princeton: Princeton University, 1998), *Movies and American Society* (Oxford: Blackwell, 2002), and *Hollywood Left and Right: How Movie Stars Shaped American Politics* (Oxford: Oxford University, 2013), which received a Film Scholars Award from the Academy of Motion Picture Arts and Sciences. The *New York Times Book Review* selected *Hollywood Left and Right* as one of its "Recommended Summer Readings" for 2012. He is currently writing *Hitler in Los Angeles: How Jews and Their Spies Foiled Nazi Plots Against Hollywood and America* (for Bloomsbury Press). Ross's Op-Ed pieces have appeared in the *Los Angeles Times, Wall Street Journal, Washington Post, Politico.com*, and the *Huffington Post*.

NORA RUBEL is the Jane and Alan Batkin Professor of Jewish Studies, Associate Professor of Religion and Classics, and the Director of the Susan B. Anthony Institute for Gender, Sexuality and Women's Studies at the University of Rochester. Trained in American Religions at the University of North Carolina-Chapel Hill, Professor Rubel teaches courses in a variety of areas including courses in American Religion and Jewish Studies. Her first book, *Doubting the Devout: The Ultra-Orthodox in the Jewish American Imagination* (Columbia University, 2009), examined the representations of religiously observant Jews in popular culture. She writes on a wide variety of topics related to religion, gender, race and ethnicity, particularly in relation to food. She is co-editor of *Religion, Food and Eating in North America* (Columbia University, 2014) and is currently completing a monograph entitled *Recipes for the Melting Pot: The Lives of The Settlement Cook Book*.

The USC Casden Institute for the Study of the Jewish Role in American Life

The American Jewish community has played a vital role in shaping the politics, culture, commerce and multiethnic character of Southern California and the American West. Beginning in the mid-nineteenth century, when entrepreneurs like Isaias Hellman, Levi Strauss and Adolph Sutro first ventured out West, American Jews became a major force in the establishment and development of the budding Western territories. Since 1970, the number of Jews in the West has more than tripled. This dramatic demographic shift has made California—specifically, Los Angeles—home to the second largest Jewish population in the United States. Paralleling this shifting pattern of migration, Jewish voices in the West are today among the most prominent anywhere in the United States. Largely migrating from Eastern Europe, the Middle East and the East Coast of the United States, Jews have invigorated the West, where they exert a considerable presence in every sector of the economy—most notably in the media and the arts. With the emergence of Los Angeles as a world capital in entertainment and communications, the Jewish perspective and experience in the region are being amplified further. From artists and activists to scholars and professionals, Jews are significantly influencing the shape of things to come in the West and across the United States. In recognition of these important demographic and societal changes, in 1998 the University of Southern California established a scholarly institute dedicated to studying contemporary Jewish life in America with special emphasis on the western United States. The Casden Institute explores issues related to the interface between the Jewish community and the broader, multifaceted cultures that form the nation—issues of relationship as much as of Jewishness itself. It is also enhancing the educational experience for students at USC and elsewhere by exposing them to the problems—and promise—of life in Los Angeles' ethnically, socially, culturally and economically diverse community. Scholars, students and community leaders examine the ongoing contributions of American Jews in the arts, business, media, literature, education, politics, law and social relations, as well as the relationships between Jewish Americans and other groups, including African Americans,

Latinos, Asian Americans and Arab Americans. The Casden Institute's scholarly orientation and contemporary focus, combined with its location on the West Coast, set it apart from—and makes it an important complement to—the many excellent Jewish Studies programs across the nation that center on Judaism from an historical or religious perspective.

For more information about the USC Casden Institute,
visit www.usc.edu/casdeninstitute, e-mail casden@usc.edu,
or call (213) 740-3405.